FUNDAMENTALS OF PUBLIC RELATIONS

Fundamentals of Public Relations

Edited by
K.B. Datta

AKANSHA PUBLISHING HOUSE
NEW DELHI - 110 002 (INDIA)

AKANSHA PUBLISHING HOUSE
R-37B, Vani Vihar, Uttam Nagar
New Delhi - 110 059
E-mail: ektabooks@yahoo.com

Showroom
4649/21-B, Ansari Road
Daryaganj, New Delhi - 110 002
Phones: 23263193, 9811582579

Fundamentals of Public Relations

First Published, 2005

ISBN 81-8370-011-X

PRINTED IN INDIA

Published by M.P. Misra for Akansha Publishing House, New Delhi - 110 059 and Printed at Tarun Offset Press, Delhi.

Contents

Preface

> "Public relations is the management function which evaluates public relations, identifies the policies and procedures of an individual or an organisation with the public interest, and plans and executes a programme of action to earn public understanding and acceptance".
>
> – *Public Relations News*

Public relations (PR), a rather new management discipline, is still an enigma to many. The media men are partly responsible for treating public relations as a frill exercise or a face-saving device employed by those who find themselves in a soup.

A clear distinction needs to be drawn between public relations and propaganda. Described as "an instrument of politics, a power for social control", Goebbels felt the aim of propaganda was not essentially to inform but to influence and not necessarily to convert but to attract followers and to keep them in line. The task of propaganda was "to blanket every area of human activity so that the environment of the individual is changed to absorb the Movement's World review". According to him in propaganda one was free to distract or even falsify them to achieve one's purpose.

Public relations in contrast recognises a long-term responsibility and aims at persuading and achieving mutual understanding and not coercing people to toe a particular line. Coined in the States in the first quarter of the 20th century, the term public relations essentially meant how a company was perceived by consumers and by the public at large. Over the years, its scope has come to encompass many publics such as employees, shareholders, bureaucracy, opinion makers, media, wholesalers, dealers, consumers, community and the people at large.

What is Public Relations? Keeping in view, the conceptual inputs gathered from definitions it is apt here to quote, Cutlip, et al. who say:

"Public Relations is a planned and sustained programme conducted by an organisation's management. It deals with the relationships between an organisation and its various constituent publics. Monitors awareness, opinions, attitudes, and behaviour inside and outside the organisation. Analyses the impact of organisational policies, procedures, and actions on various publics. Adjusts those policies, procedures and actions found to be in conflict with the public interest and organisational survival. Counsels management on the establishment of new policies, procedures, and actions that are mutually beneficial to the organisation and its publics. Establishes and maintains two-way communication between the organisation and its various publics. Produces specific changes in awareness, opinions, attitudes, and behaviour inside and outside the organisation. Results in new and/or maintained relationships between an organisation and its publics."

Does this sound high tech? Or an exercise in intangibles? Certainly not. Every single constituent group whose opinion has a bearing on the survival of an organisation can be identified to precision. Public Relations as a channel for effective communication can be put to action with definable and quantifiable objectives which could be measured to assess the impact.

Public relations has a vast potential of employment. A PRO is an ambassdor of his/her organisation. Image building, goodwill creation, making publics aware of policies and programmes etc. are his jobs. Basically, it is a management function being performed with journalistic professionalism and approach.

The Public Relations practitioner has also to study the media habits and communication behaviour of these men. In other words he has to gather data about their world and their media habits to select the appropriate media channels to reach out to them. In brief, we have to keep in view the message, the medium and the target audience if we are to influence the minds of certain groups to make them feel positively inclined to buy or subscribe our product, idea or service. Similarly for a political party, its target audience will not only include those voters who owe allegiance to their ideology, but also those who are fence sitters, the ones who are indecisive but could respond with persuasive propositions and also voters supposedly loyal to other political parties. As in advertising and publicity, in public relations also three things (3 W's) are important, e.g., *what* you say to *whom* and *where*.

This book on Public Relations, is compilation of valuable information based on authoritative sources. We have tried to highlight all salient features of Public Relations in pros and cons. The book is devised on painstaking research of many experts in the field. And source of information are all secondary i.e., books, reports, journals, magazines, articles, research papers, etc. As such entire credit for this goes to them whose works and views are subscribed.

We express our gratefulness to different authors and experts for sharing their views by way of citation or otherwise. Officials of different libraries, friends and nears and dears deserve our appreciation and we are deeply beholden to them all. Last but not the least we owe a deep sense of thankfulness to Mr. M.P. Misra for bringing out this book within very short span of time.

We will feel amply rewarded if this could help those for whom this is meant.

–KBD

1

Introduction to Public Relations: History, Principles & Functions

I

'Public relations' (PR) though a new term in usage, has been in application since very ancient times. It is worth to be mentioned that in India during some 300 B.C., King Ashoka prepared his famous edicts that were set up on pillars in different parts of his empire. The inscriptions were meant to inform the people about the policies of his government, to persuade them to carry out certain tasks and to create goodwill amongst them. The Ashokan inscriptions were in the local script. Thus, those found in the north-west are in the Kharoshthi script derived from the Aramaic script used in Persia. At the extreme west of the empire, near modern Kandahar (Afghanistan), the inscriptions are in Greek and, Aramaic elsewhere in India they are in the Brahmi script. Evidently this is not only an example of public relations but of a fairly developed form and sense of it which takes into account the need, to approach various sections of the people in their own languages.

Public relations as we understand it today is something rather different. It is a phenomenon that has emerged in modern society because of the nature of that society, the nature of the social, political and economic institutions that have been developed in the world today and the behaviour of different groups of people within society.

While its genesis may be a matter of historical interest, to try to compare the business or the science of public relations as practised today with the type of communications represented by the inscriptions of Ashoka would be like trying to compare a sailing vessel with a modern watercraft.

Introduction

Virtually, it may be useful to begin by first getting out of the way certain popular notions which, as with many popular beliefs, are either without any basis in reality or at best express only half truths. For instance, public relations personnel are regarded by some to be fixers, a breed of people who will wangle things for you by the most questionable methods. There is also a popular idea that Public Relations professionals spend most of their time 'wining and dining', using for the purpose fabulous expense accounts they are supposed to have access to. While no one can prevent a charlatan from posing as a Public Relations man or styling himself as a Public Relations consultant he is no more a true practitioner of Public Relations than a quack selling magic remedies by the wayside is a physician.

Often, Public Relations is confused with publicity. Publicity is certainly one of the instruments of Public Relations but it would be as wrong to equate publicity with Public Relations just as it would be to equate the stethoscope with the practice of modern medicine. To continue the analogy Public Relations seeks to diagnose the ills of art organisation in its relations with the public or any segment, of the public, it prescribes remedies and proceeds to administer them, It then; keeps a watch, on the patient to see whether the remedies prescribed are producing the desired effect so that the medicine can be changed if necessary after evaluating the results. Again, as in medicine prevention is considered more important than the cure. Public Relations believes in maintaining the good health of the corporate body so that drastic remedies and bitter pills may not have to be gulped afterwards.

Public Relations which is now a well-established discipline therefore needs to be defined so that we may be clear about what we are discussing when we talk about PR. A definition, however, is not easy and different authorities approaching the subject from different ends have come out with their own definitions on PR. Edward L. Bernays defines it as 'the attempt by information, persuasion and adjustment to engineer public support for an activity, cause, movement or institution'.

Professor Edward J. Robinson defines Public Relations as: 'Public relations as and applied social and behavioural science is that function which—(1) measures, evaluates and interprets the attitudes of various relevant publics; (2) assists management in defining objectives for increasing public understanding and acceptance of the organisation's products, plans, policies and personnel; (3) equates these objectives with the interests, needs and goals of the various relevant publics; and (4) develops, executes and evaluates a programme to earn public understanding and acceptance.'

Sam Black in *Practical Public Relations* says that, 'the fundamental purpose of public relations practice is to establish a two-way flow of mutual understanding based on truth, knowledge and full information.'

The well-known journal *Public Relations News*, edited by Denny Griswold, defines Public Relations as follows: "Public Relations is the management function which evaluates public attitudes, identifies the policies and procedures of an individual or an organisation with the public interest, and plans and executes a programme of action to earn public understanding and acceptance."

The Institute of Public Relations (UK). devoted prolonged attention to this problem and the result of their exercise yielded a definition which now generally finds, favour with Public Relations practitioners in many parts of the world including the majority of practitioners in India. According to the Institute, Public Relations practice is defined as 'the deliberate, planned and sustained effort to establish and maintain mutual understanding between an organisation and its public".

What is the Necessity of Public Relations?

The need for Public Relations is inherent in the very nature of modern society and people can ignore it only at their great loss. Society is made up of many groups of people, each with its own interests—interests which are different from and in some cases even in conflict with the interests of other groups. Sometimes the same person may reflect different views depending on which interest group he is representing at a given moment. Thus as a consumer one may be interested in holding the price line. As a manager responsible for the profitability of a business enterprise one may wish to initiate measures that would lead to a general price rise. This kind of a society, made up of different groups of people with different interests, is referred to as a pluralistic society. The harmonious functioning of a pluralistic society clearly needs the help of organised Public Relations.

In the modern world the public has become a force to be reckoned with. Even, in a country where the majority is still to acquire the rudiments of literacy, people are conscious of their rights as citizens as, consumers, as shareholders or as employees. What is more, they are no longer dumb driven cattle but can make their voice heard.

Modern society has given birth to institutions that

make it possible for the common man to make his presence felt. If he has a grievance he can write a letter to the editor of a popular daily or weekly. He can go up to his MLA or MP or his local councillor other representative.

The following can be publics for a modern business organisation can:

(a) Government;
(b) Shareholders;
(c) Municipalities and other Local Bodies;
(d) Central Parliament and the State Legislatures;
(e) Dealers;
(f) Customers;
(g) Press;
(h) Suppliers;
(j) Organisation's own employees; and
(j) Community around.

A Managerial Tool

Despite the fact that Public Relations today is now formally accepted, there is very little appreciation of the potentiality of this discipline in achieving management objectives and yet there is hardly any area of top management functioning where considerations of public relations do not enter, hardly any aspect of management policy that does not have a Public Relations angle. This is even more so in India where there is an undercurrent of hostility to business among the people at large. Success is suspect and profit is nowhere regarded so: much, a duty word as in India.

This is partly due perhaps to India's tradition. In Indian society materialism is frowned, upon and renunciation of the worlds is encouraged. The natural suspicion of people in respect of business has been strengthened by the role that some unscrupulous businessmen and traders, have played by hoarding and profiteering and taking advantage of shortages of essential commodities to make quick profits. Business in India, therefore, can least of all ignore the role of public relations. Any business organisation which tries to function today without understanding fully the environment in which it is functioning and the changes that are taking place in it is bound to end up in disaster.

This is true anywhere in the world and again perhaps more so in Indian conditions where the environment is even more complex than in the developed countries and subject to sudden changes. The maintenance of a proper public relations set-up will help a management to understand and also to anticipate environmental changes which are likely to have a bearing on the functioning of the organisation. It will enable the concerned organisation to prepare itself for the required changes.

Public relations can play a role in developing favourable equations with each of the various publics or segments of the public with which it is concerned. To cite the instance of capital market, any organisation which is not government-owned depends on the market for raising capital or to some extent for raising loans. The response to any call for equity or debentures will depend on the reputation of the organisation in the financial market. An organisation that has neglected the vital task of communicating with existing or potential shareholders will find to its dismay that its calls for money remain unheeded. The customers are another vital section of. the public with which the organisation is concerned. Here, too, public relations can play a role. When you are launching a new product, your work is more than half done if your organisation has established a reputation for quality and reliability. If that reputation has been, established it is enough for the public to know that the product *A* is coming from the company X towards which the public is favourably inclined. One can easily extend this line of though to appreciate how important the record and reputation of a company is in its relations with the press, the government, the legislators etc.

Some examples may be cited to show the effectiveness of using Public Relations techniques in solving complicated problems that face industry. Both these examples are from real life and represent the experience of companies functioning in India.

Now take a case of a company Z which was faced with a serious problem of inter-union rivalry. The conflict reached such a state that there was a complete stoppage of work in the industry as each one of the unions insisted that they should be given recognition as a precondition for giving the call for resumption of work and since leaders of both groups had pockets of influence in the industry, between them they succeeded in paralysing the functioning of the organisation. The top management of the company realised the complexity of the problem and came to the conclusion that the normal procedure of asking for Government help to resolve the dispute would not by itself lead to a solution. The Public Relations Department was called in and a programme was worked out. The essence of the strategy was to use the press and other media extensively to rouse public opinion and bring pressure on the leaders of both groups to call off the stoppage of work. This was done by issuing daily press releases bringing out the effects of the stoppage of work on various vital sectors of industry with which this company was connected.

Simultaneously persona contacts were established with

the industrial correspondents of leading newspapers and the situation was explained to them. By impressing upon them the gravity of the situation and the serious damage that was being, caused by a continuation of the deadlock they were persuaded to write feature articles and editorials commenting on the absurdity of prolonging a strike merely to resolve an inter-union dispute. The weight of public opinion as expressed in the press had its impact. Simultaneously personal contacts were established with. Government officials and Ministers and they were also persuaded to bring pressure on the union leaders. The cumulative effect of this was that resumption of work became possible within a short time. There is a case of another company Z which found its costs were goings up as a result of excessive wastage in production. Here again, the management realised that the best method of dealing with the situation was to call in the Public Relations Department to play a role. The Public Relations Department of the organisation studied, the problem and devised a campaign using various media of mass communication within the organisation to impress upon the workers the necessity to eliminate wastage. As a result of a sustained campaign there was a considerable drop in the wastage and as a consequence a significant lowering of costs.

It is to be noted here that if public relations is to be effective it is essential that the closest rapport should exist between the top management and the Public Relations setup of the organisation. The Public Relations department should be fully aware of top level management thinking and planning. It is only where this is so that Public Relations will be able to advise management effectively on whether its thinking and planning is in tune with public moods and aspirations. Public Relations can be most effective where it not only has access to top management and is able to get information from it but has an actual role to play in the making and implementation of policies.

Public Relations Abroad: Development Scenario

Bernays states: "Only one week after the United States entered World War I, on April 6, 1917, the Committee on Public Information was set up under the direction of George Creel, former editor of *Rocky Mountain News.* Other members were the Secretaries of War, Navy and State. The United States Committee on Public Information had two sections: foreign and domestic. It functioned, until June 30, 1919. One of the very potent factors in its organisation was the, fact, that Creel was close to Wilson and that government action at high policy levels was coordinated with the propaganda. I worked with the Committee on Public Information in the United States and Paris. I saw it grow from an idea to an organisation of enthusiastic men and women in key centres throughout the world. They used the aptitudes and skills they had to further a better knowledge everywhere of the war aims and ideas of the United States. This experience in board public relations was a turning point in the lives of those who worked the Committee."

Likewise developments were taking place in other countries of the world. Under various names departments of information or propaganda which were essential for carrying out a public relations function were operating in Germany, France and Britain. Towards the close of World War I, came the Russian Revolution of 1917. The Soviet Government and the Communist International used the weapon of propaganda even more intensively and directed a flow of communication to all corners of the world that was to have a drastic impact on the political situation in many countries of the world.

However, it was in the United States of America (USA), that developments took place which converted the vague propaganda and publicity drives into organised and scientific public relations. From the end of World War I to the stock market crash in 1929, basic trends and events hastened the development of public relations.

Bernays describes how the term 'public relations' came to be used to describe the type of activity that he and some other pioneers in the field of public relations such as Ivy Lee were carrying on in the United States at that time. Ivy Lee who was also working in this field at that time used various terms to define his organisation—publicity adviser, publicity expert, publicity director, profession of publicity. A bulletin published by Ivy Lee and Associates in 1921 was titled Public Relations. The period from 1929 to 1941 was marked by tremendous changes in the USA and in the world. The stock market crash of 1929 rocked a the country. The depression that followed was USA's greatest economic crisis. President Hoover entered the White House in 1929 as the symbol of prosperity he left it in 1933 as the symbol of debacle. He was followed by President Franklin Roosevelt, who occupied the White House's for twelve years. Profound economic, social and political changes in America and around the globe took place, accompanied by propaganda, publicity and public relations on an unprecedented scale.

Business now realised that in addition to selling its products under unfavourable conditions of economic decline, it needed also and above all to sell itself to the public, to explain its contributions to the entire economic system. Business recognised that if it did not do so, conflicting ideas might abolish or modify business itself. Then too, the increasing attention given by universities, publicists and writers to the importance of sound public relations made business aware of the need for modifying its attitudes and actions, to conform to public demands.

In 1938, *Fortune,* the business magazine took congizance of public relations for the first time since the founding of the magazine three years earlier. The October issue included an article which pointed out that America's favourite subject of attack was business. The American people, *Fortune* said, had never really been sold on business, particularly of the modern, industrial variety. 'Now the supposed cure for this situation', the article continued, 'is what the businessman calls public relations. The term is a broad one and may include all sorts of promotional activity, from commercial advertising to after-dinner speeches.

As such the period from 1929 to 1941 marked a great turning point in the history of public relations. Through the work of individual public relations counsels, through a developing literature, through university courses, through widespread discussions in the lay, trade, business, and scientific press, and through the increasing .use of professional public: relations guidance by government, business, labour, medicine; and other segments of society, the new profession was not only growing but also broadening and deepening its outlook.

By 1940, Europe was already engaged in World War II. By the summer of 1941, the armed forces became keenly interested in public relations. In World War II, the emphasis in public relations was, as in World War I, on winning the war. But since 1917 public relations had developed new methods and techniques, the orientation of the public was different, too. Many factors had to be considered in these new activities and approaches to the public. Technical tools had still further speeded up communication— radio, sound film, air travel. The United State of America was fighting totalitarian States—Germany, Italy, Japan. These conditions allowed government public relations to make a far greater impact than during the earlier war. The office of War Information in the US and the thousands of public relations officers in the armed services provided machinery to carry forward the basic ideas. The importance of public relations having been accepted and appreciated during World War II, business realised the need to take over its techniques and use them to improve its own image. There were enough indications that in the post-war world the public was still suspicious of it. A survey of public relations made by *Fortune* magazine in its May 1949 issue, for example, was captioned "Business is Still in Trouble: only good public relations," i.e., good performance that's understood and appreciated will ensure its future'. *Fortune* then gave a definition, a history, and a present analysis of public relations, ending with the warning that 'either the day of public relations as performance must come or private business must reconcile itself to a steady contracting. American business still has time to meet the challenge of our time. It can effect the people a generous measure of both security and opportunity'.

Dr. Scott Cutlip feels that public relations in the United States began as early as the sixteenth century. Discussing the history of Public Relations in America he says:

> "American Public Relations began in the 16th century when Sir Walter Raleigh is said to have persuaded people to settle in rural Virginia. In the 18th century poineers moving Westwards, were carving out land settlements using the aid of publicity. The first intensive organised, systematic effort to win and mobilise public opinion came with the American Revolution. The revolution was not a mass spontaneous uprising of all the people, it was nurtured and successfully brought about by a very small band of dedicated propagandists, led by Sa Adams who

developed the slogan "No Taxation Without Representation".

"The next stage came with the American Constitution. Our Declaration of Independence is a Public Relations document, written out of a decent respect for the opinions of mankind. The next big crisis came with the American Civil. War in which both sides were well represented to the public through PR.

"PR in the modern sense began to develop in the 1880's and 1890's on a fairly extensive scale because this was the beginning of American industrialisation. Through the next 25 years the nation expanded with communication requirements and facilities.'

"The 1896 Presidential campaign marked a turning point in our political life. It was the first modern Presidential campaign and this was not accidental. In 1952, the Presidential campaigns began to change with the advent of television. By the turn of the 19th century the power of publicity in the business and commercial world was clear. Public Relations as a concept of management and specialised vocation is essentially a 20th century development. The development of Public Relations in the United States in the 20th century can be divided into five distinct periods."

According to Dr. Scott Cutlip the first phase of public relations in the modern sense was the period, between 1900 and 1917 which he calls the seed-bed years of the Public Relations profession in the United States. The next phase from 1917 onwards was the stage of World-War I. Public Relations activities during this period have been elaborated sufficiently in the account given by Bernays. The next phase 1923-1933 was the period of economic depression. During this period social responsibility began to acquire a hold over business for a number of reasons, both economic and political. Public Relations functions, therefore, developed even further.

Again from 1933 to World War II, was a period of great growth in PR. Public Relations also made its impact on university education and became a university discipline. People had to be formally educated in it. The Public Relations News was started in 1944 and the Public Relations Journal in the same year.

In 1969 the American Public Relations Association, a small Washington-based group merged in the Public Relations Society of America (PRSA). The PRSA is now the general professional Public Relations organisation and has more than 6,000 members.

Public relations has continually tried to emphasise that business cannot survive without public support and that support cannot come by mere press agentry or gimmickry. It has to be based on performance, on solid achievement, on the conscious effort to fulfil social responsibility and to identify private interest with the public good. Every lapse on the part of some business organisation is followed by new efforts to develop stricter codes and norms of conduct for business corporations and so on.

Code for MNC

Of late,revelations concerning a number of large corporations which function throughout the world have done further damage to the reputation of business. Firms like ITT, Lockheed, Gulf Oil and others have been found to be guilty of trying to subvert the governments of some of the countries in which they have operated outlying to achieve their objectives by recourse to bribery, of local governments officials on a massive scale. These revelations have given rise to a wave of protest throughout the world and many companies are now working out codes of conduct for their employees to prevent recourse to such practices. The United

Nations is also working on some kind, of code for multinational corporations while the Organisation for Economic Cooperation and Development (OECD) has already announced such a code after much debate.

The OECD code recommends that multinational companies operating in OECD countries:

'take fully into account' governments' policy objectives; provide subsidiaries with information the local government may ask for taking into account 'legitimate requirements' of business confidentiality;

not bribe, make illegal political contributions or become improperly involved in local politics;

allow subsidiaries freedom to develop and sell at home and abroad, consistent with the need for specialisation and sound commercial practice;

with due regard to confidentiality and cost, publish information about: their structure; holdings in (and cross-holdings between) affiliates; geographical areas (as defined by the company) where they work and what they do there; operating results, sales and new capital investment by geographical area; sales and, as far as practicable, new investment by major lines of business; intragroup pricing policies;

not abuse dominant market positions by, e.g. anticompetitive takeover, unreasonable refusal to deal, discriminatory pricing or using such pricing within the group so as to harm competitors;

not take part 'in anticompetitive cartels, unless these are within the law;

cooperate in antitrust investigations;

allow purchasers, distributors and licencees freedom to develop and sell—consistent with law, trade conditions, need for specialisation; and sound commercial practice not modify (e.g. by fiddling transfer prices) in ways contrary to national laws the tax base on which members of the group are assessed;

respect employees' right to unionise, negotiate with their representatives and provide these with the information needed for serious negotiations;

also provide them with information enabling them to obtain a true and fair view of the company's (subsidiary, or, 'where appropriate', the whole group) performance — where this accords with local law and practice;

at least match the employment and labour-relations standards of comparable employers in the host country;

not threaten, in the context of labour negotiations, to transfer operations elsewhere;

provide employees with reasonable notice of major changes such as closures, and do their practicable best to mitigate the adverse effects;

not discriminate in employment, unless this is in furtherance of government policies which promote greater equality of employment opportunity.

Now, Public relations practitioners in the entire world where public relations is recognised as a profession have come together in various national bodies or associations to improve their professional skills and also to try collectively to influence corporate practice and to ensure that business works in harmony with the public interest in general.

International Public Relations Association

The concept of an international public relations body came into being in 1949 when, two Dutch and three British public relations men met in London. As they talked of their work they developed the idea of organising public relations people into a para-national society, the objective of which would be to raise the standard of public relations practice in the various countries and improve the professional quality and efficiency of public relations practitioners.

Later in the ensuing year a group public relations

executives from France, Great Britain, the Netherlands, Norway, and the United States of America, met in Holland under the auspices of the Royal Netherlands International Trade Fair, and the Public Relations Society of Holland. After discussion, these pioneers issued a signed statement to the effect that having 'considered the necessity of furthering the skill and ethics of their profession, and of a clearer understanding of their work, and having considered further the value of international exchange of information and co-operation' they 'resolved that a Provisional International Committee be set up with the object of promoting such exchange and co-operation—and the eventual establishment of an International Public Relations Association.' Several members of the Dutch Public Relations Society endorsed this document within twenty-four hours of its issue.

An ad-hoc International Committee was formed and during the next five years meetings were held in England—usually in conjunction with the annual week-end Conference of the British Institute of Public Relations. These meetings were attended by representatives from France, United Kingdom, the Netherlands, Norway and the United States of America together with observers from Australia, Belgium, Canada, Finland, Italy and Switzerland. The International Public Relations Association (IPRA) was officially established in London on 1 May 1955. The IPRA Council has met annually to execute the affairs of the Association, and to consider ways of implementing research carried out by the Standing Committees.

One early achievement of the organisation was the adoption of a 'Code of Conduct' for the purpose of estabushing standards of professional ethics and conduct in the field of public relations for all members, of the Association worldwide. The IPRA Code of Conduct, which, was adopted at the Venice Meeting in, 1961, has. served as a basis for the formulation of a number of new codes for recently established national public relations associations and societies.

The 'Code of Athens' an International Code of Ethics exemplifying public relations as a foundation for dialogue— was adopted by the IPRA Council at its 1965 Meeting in Athens. The Code of Athens is IPRA's "moral charter", its principles being inspired by the United Nations Declaration of Human Rights.

Nine World Congresses (held every three years) have been sponsored by IPRA with the following themes: Public Relations in the Service of Mankind (Brussels 1958); Public Relations for the Progress of the Community—Experience and Methods (Venice 1961); Public Relations and the Tides of Change (Montreal 1964); Public Relations and the New Demands of a Changing World (Rio de Janeiro-1967); Public Relations—The Bridge to International Understanding (Tel Aviv 1970); Public Relations—A Profession Comes of Age (Geneva 1973); Public Relations in the Parliament of Man (Boston 1976); Challenges of a Changing World (London 1979); The Interdependent World (Bombay 1982); and Between People and Power (Amsterdam 1985). The last World Congress was held in Melbourne in 1988 and had as its theme 'Values in Communications'. The Association has been developing substantially and numerically over the years and has become a professional and fraternal organisation which now unites more than 800 leading public relations practitioners in 62 countries.

Every Education and training have been one of the main preoccupations of IPRA since its foundation. The Gold Paper which is. published at the time of the World Congress was in 1982 entitled 'A Model for Public Relations

Education for Professional Practice and adopted in many world, centres of learning. The Gold Paper in 1985 bore the title 'The Communicative Society' a new era in human history.

In 1973, the first formal link was established between national. and international public relations associations when a Council of Presidents of National, Regional and International Associations was created through the agency of IPRA. In 1974, IPRA held its first meeting in India—prior to the Fourth All-India Public Relations Conference. In 1975, IPRA sponsored the First All-Africa Public Relations Conference (9-13 June) in Nairobi, Kenya, and thus demonstrated the growth of public relations in Africa. The creation of the Federation of African Public Relations Association (FAPRA) was a dramatic outcome of the Conference which brought African practitioners from widely separated countries together for the first time. The First Seminar jointly sponsored by the International Public Relations Association (IPRA) and the United Nations Environment Programme (UNEP) further contributed to bring about global recognition of the Profession. The IPRA UNEP Seminar, entitled 'The Mediterranean Community-Laboratory for Survival', was held in Athens, Greece, on 26 November 1975, and was the first of its kind to take place in the Mediterranean area.

Public Relations in India: Historical Development

In the absence of reliable data it is difficult to delineate a clear-cut history of Public Relations in India. While a formal history may be of interest in the academic sense, for an understanding of the problems of Public Relations in India, it is not really very relevant. What is more relevant is to see the different stages that have taken place in the development of Public Relations in India.

Stages of Development

Though viewed from different angles, the development of Public Relations can be grouped under four phases:

(i) The early stage where Public Relations was practised less as a matter of deliberate Public Relations policy and more out of a liberal and philanthropic approach or out of sheer necessity for disseminating information. This stage continued till the World War II;

(ii) The next stage started during the World War II and can be defined as a stage of conscious PR. This stage still continues but a further development took place in the post-independence period specially towards the latter half of the fifties and the early half of the sixties;

(iii) The third stage of Public Relations is thus represented by the response of organisations in India to the new environment created in the wake of the Government's Industrial Policy Resolution and the growth of democratic institutions in India — Parliament, the Legislatures, etc.

(iv) The fourth stage is represented by what one may call the stage of professionalism in Public Relations when Public Relations practitioners began to organise themselves as a professional body and tried to develop their skills as Public Relations people. It was in this period that the Public Relations Society of India began to play an active role and initiated a movement to improve standards of Public Relations practice in India.

The First Stage

The early stage of public relations referred to as the stage before conscious Public Relations actrvity started arose out of the efforts made by liberal and philanthropic industrial pioneers and also out of certain pressing needs for dissemination of information. Two notable examples of this type of public relations may be cited the public relations and more specifically the community relations practised by the house of Tatas and the public relations in the Railaways. In India the Tata Iron and steel Company went into production in 1912. From the very begining the house of Tata started practising community relations by building Jamshedpur as a model township. Besides providing housing, water, electric supply and free primary education, the company runs a hospital and also a technical institute which was established as early as 1921. The company also promotes social, cultural and economic development of the community.

Again, in the Railways public relations efforts in the pre-World War II period were perhaps dictated by commercial needs. Having built the railways at considerable cost mainly for the purpose of carrying raw materials from the hinterland to the ports the private companies who were then running the railways realised that without promoting passenger traffic the railways would not be commercially viable. It is understood that in the early twenties the GIP Railway in India carried on a public relations campain in England to attract tourists to India using the media of advertising and pamphlets. Within the country the Publicity Bureau of this railway introduced a travelling cinema which gave open-air shows of the films at fairs and festivals. Subsequently publicity officers with similar, functions were extended to other railways. The Railway Board established publicity bureaus in London and New York too. It is understood that both the London and New York offices used to advertise extensively in newspapers and journals. Both these offices participated in exhibitions held abroad to popularise Indian Railways and attract tourists traffic.

One more form of public relations that was practised directly by the Government started as early as the World War I when the Government of India felt it necessary to disseminate information and to have an organisation to feed the press and to supply war news to the people. A Central Publicity Board was established and subsequently Sir Stanley Reed, Editor of *The Times of India,* Mumbai, was asked to work as the Chairman. The Board had on it representatives from the army and the foreign and the political departments of the Government of India. After the end of the war the function, of this Board was taken over by the Central Bureau, of Information which was established in 1921 and Prof. Rushbrook William from Allahabad was invited to become its first Director. In 1923 the Central Bureau was redesignated as the Directorate of Public Instruction. Later, this was renamed as the Directorate of Information and Broadcasting.

The Second Stage of Conscious Public Relations

The stage of conscious Public Relations is the second stage. This, development took place because certain objective factors had arisen in the environment which gave rise to the need for deliberate Public Relations activity.

The responsible factors were:

(a) the emergence of a vocal public opinion;
(b) the emergence of mass circulated newspapers and an influential press;
(c) outbreak of the Second World War and the need for mobilising public opinion in favour of the war effort.

To meet the needs of the situation arising out of the Second World War, particularly the need to mobilise public opinion in favour of the war effort in a situation where the Indian National Congress and national sentiment generally were against the war effort, the Government took a number of measures. A Ministry of Information and Broadcasting was created and the Directorate of Information which had earlier been formed was amalgamated while the new Ministry. The main function of the newly created Ministry of Information was to create public opinion in the country in favour of the war effort. Opinion had also to be created in favour of such measures as recruitment of the Defence Forces, price control and rationing of foodgrains. There were a number of units under this Ministry such as the War purposes Exhibition Unit the Films Division and the Central Bureau of Public Opinion. Just, as on a world-scale and Europe it was mainly the need for mobilising public opinion in favour of the war effort that gave an impetus to organised public relations activities in the World War I so also in India at the time the World War II. It was in this period, too that certain industrial houses which had already been practising public, relations on a spontaneous basis began: to organise their Public Relations activity in a conscious way. The house of Tatas formed a public relations department at their Head Office in Bombay in 1943. Publication of a monthly News Bulletin was started in 1944.

The Third Stage

Infact, the third stage of Public Relations may be said to have started with, the coming of Independence to the country. There was a completely new environment and new political institutions. Some of the salient features of the new environment were: .

(a) the emergence of Parliament and the State Legislatures elected for the first time on the basis of adult franchise;

(b) the adoption by the Government of the Industrial Policy Resolution and the Industrial (Development and Regulation) Act.

Having based of these factors both Government and business organisations had to adopt conscious and deliberate policies of public relations. It is from this period that Public Relations practice in the modern sense of the term began in India.

Multinational companies which already had their own expertise in public relations as it had developed in the United States and Europe began to make use of these techniques so that they may be able to survive and grow in the post-Independence environment. In the fifties and the early sixties companies like Burmah-Shell, Esso, Caltex, Dunlop, Philips, Hindustan Levers and Indian Oxygen set up departments to execute programmes of public relations to meet the new situation. Indian companies, also began to set up their own public relations departments to carry on organised Public Relations activity.

The Fourth Stage

Professionalism in PR: The fourth stage by the emergence of professionalism in Public Relations which started with the formation of professional organisations of Public Relations practitioners in various parts of India notably in Mumbai and Kolkata. The Public Relations Society of India was formed in Mumbai as early as 1958. A few years later a Chapter of the Public Relations Society was organised in Kolkata. Prior to this a Public Relations Circle had functioned in Calcutta. As early as 1960 a Public Relations course was organised by Tata Steel's PRO and it was held under the auspices of the Calcutta Management Association at the Bengal Chamber of Commerce Offices. These were however, localised efforts and the first all-India effort to win recognition for Public Relations as a profession was made with the holding of the first Public Relations Conference in New Delhi in April 1968. This Conference took note of the fact that while public relations had been gaining currency the reputation of the profession was sullied by the fact that a large number of people were masquerading as public relations practitioners who were in reality nothing better than fixers and lobbyists of various kinds often operating with the most dubious of methods. Understandably, therefore, the concern of the first conference was the discussion and adoption of a code of ethics and some attempt to define the parameters of the public relations profession.

The start given to the Public Relations movement by the first Public Relations Conference set it off on the right track. Since then it has matured and developed. Periodic conferences have been organised under the auspices of the Public Relations Society of India to take stock of developments in the field and to enable Public Relations practitioners to share their experiences with one another. The second. Public Relations Conference was held in Chinnai in 1972 and was mainly concerned with the status and functions of public relations in the management hierarchy. The third was held in Calcutta in 1972 and had as its theme: "PR in the changing environment. The fourth all-India conference was held in Bombay in 1974 on the theme: "Towards a more responsible citizenship". A meeting of the Council of the International Public Relations Association (IPRA) was synchronised with this conference and this helped to expose practitioners in India to the experience of other parts of the world. "Towards greater professionalism"—a very down to earth topic was the theme of the fifth all-India Public Relations Conference held in New Delhi in 1976. This was followed by a conference in Cochin in 1978 which had as its theme. The next conference coincided with the Ninth World Public Relations Congress and was held in Mumbai in 1982 on the themme—"The interdependent world".

Since then many All-India Public Relations conferences have been held.

The 13th Conference to be held at Bengalore on the theme: "Change—A challenge for PR" had just been announced when this book went to the press. The growing participation and the increasing, sophistication of the presentations made at these conferences is a measure of the strides the Public Relations movement has taken in the, course of the fast two decades.

Thus, the public relations movement in India has thus travelled a long way since the early days when it was fighting for recognition as a profession, when it was regarded only as a junior partner of publicity and tended to be ignored and, when noticed at all, ridiculed rather than appreciated. Peeping through these achievements one may find some cause for satisfaction at the progress that has been registered but there can certainly be no room for complacency. While leadership in government and industry has accepted at least theoretically that public relations is one of the important tools of modern management and that public relations in the true sense of the term is a more a social science than some sort of a gimmick, old attitudes towards public relations and its practitioners persist.

II

PUBLIC RELATIONS AND OTHER MANAGEMENT DISCIPLINES

Public relations is a top management function. In order to be effective, the public relations practitioner should ideally report to the Chief Executive Officer (CEO). According to Scott M. Cutlip and others, "one of the few safe generalisations on this subject is that an organisation's public reputation derives in substantial part from its senior officials. As those with administrative responsibility and authority act and speak, so go the interpretation and echoes created by the public relations function. Public relations is inescapably tied, by nature and by necessity, to the management function". In the military context, the staff officers present studies of the various possibilities, and based, on them the line staff take action. There is, in other words, a water-tight compartmentalisation of work situation. In organisational situations, however, specially problem solving areas, staff executives work in close collaboration with line managers to make decisions. Depending on the seniority and calibre of public relations staff, their job is determined within and outside the organisation. There is, in fact, no model communication organisation. It depends upon circumstances which vary from organisation to organisation.

In some organisations, a public relations setup may have emerged after a crisis situation to deal with different publics with appropriate messages. The Public Relations people get regularised if they perform well. In such situations, their role is of "fire fighting" — in other words, "programmed" action. In other organisations, a public relations department is created as a deliberate effort with set objectives. They work by the principle of "management by objectives and results". A public relations manager's primary function is to act as a catalyst or change agent within a company. In order to fulfil this job requirement, a public relations department needs information. In a rigid or closed organisation, it is difficult to get information. The person in charge of communication is resisted because his job is to share information. In contrast, an open organisation believes in a frank and forthright two-way flow of communication.

In order to speak for and on behalf of the organisation, the public relations department must know the organisation thoroughly. In an open organisation, and specially where the Public Relations manager is taken in high esteem for his capabilities, he can even be privy to boardroom secrets. The job hence will be to evaluate the strengths, weaknesses, opportunities and threats (SWOT) facing the organisation. Here are some postulates:

1. PR has an advisory role towards the top management about internal and external development that are likely to affect the reputation of the organisation.
2. The Public Relations department should ideally be involved in organisational intelligence. The work will entail environment scanning. Even before a product is launched in the market place, it is very important to know the market forces, the perceptions of the target consumers, the competitors' strengths and weaknesses, the potential for real and stimulated demand and the mood of the opinion makers, decision makers and the fourth estate vis-a-vis the organisation.

   All this forms part of environment scanning and monitoring. Information thus gathered through primary and secondary data collection and corporate surveillance is analysed, sifted, processed and brought within the organisation for decision making at appropriate levels.

3. It must create necessary avenues within the organisation in different line and staff departments for seeking information for communication and identifying the communication needs of individual departments. For example, the finance department may have the need to communicate with the shareholders, the engineering department may be planning to make the line staff in the assembly line aware of safety precautions about self and the plant. In such and similar cases, the public relations department can advise and assist the concerned departments by writing, publishing brochures and manuals, or by making films and other audio-visual communication aids depending upon the individual needs and requirements.
4. Similarly, Public Relations should organise image surveys within and outside the organisation to gauge the people's perception about the organisation, the product or the service and to put up the findings to the management to facilitate decision making for corrective measures.
5. The Public Relations department has to identify and establish contacts with a cross-section of important external publics, encompassing decision makers, opinion makers, the media, consumer protection groups, wholesalers/retailers, specialist groups etc.
6. It is also a Public Relations job to create channels for effective flow of communication to selected publics.

7. It is necessary for Public Relations to create an emergency communication plan which should form part of the disaster management plan of the organisation.
8. Last but not the least, another job is to help establish a Public Relations environment within the company whereby people feel free to give vent to their feelings at appropriate forums and not fall victim to grapevine. In fact, the public relations department should prevent the creating of communication vacuums which, if not filled by official sources, will be filled by gossip and unauthorised sources.

Interface with Other Disciplines

The varying perceptions are a cause of occasional friction between Public Relations and other departments. This is unfortunate, since each function of the Public Relations needs the support and cooperation of the other departments for the smooth discharge of obligation of the Public Relations and other departments. In this background, let us see PR's interface with major line and staff departments.

Marketing

Marketing is all about products and people. As they reach out to the consumer, marketing people feel they are also in the business of public relations. The major area of conflict is advertising and publicity, specially product advertising and institutional advertising. In non-profit organisations, the cause of friction is the allocation of funds, raising funds and reaching out to a variety of publics with educational messages.

An institutional advertising campaign for a corporate sector company to enhance the goodwill of the organisation would need the expertise of an advertising agency, but as the primary aim is to push not a product but the company, it will fall in the arena of the Public Relations department. Conversely, publicity about products and services aimed to increase sales or use is a part of the marketing function, but because public relations people are trained in the field and are more skilled at writing and placing publicity, the function generally falls in their purview. In some major corporate organisations in the private and 'public "sectors" tire work is divided by assigning product advertising to marketing and institutional advertising to the PR. Unless, however, there is integration in communication, they are bound to go different ways. This at times gives wrong signals to the target consumer. To illustrate, a company may have launched a new product in the market, and a vigorous advertising campaign is on to woo the consumers, but on the other hand the public relations department is issuing press releases about other aspects of the company which appear in the newspapers which also carry the product ad without giving special reference to the newly launched product.

Personnel, HRD, Industrial Relations

Both Public Relations and personnel deal with employees, hence the risk of friction is high. The employees are governed by certain policies and procedures and are bound by certain personnel rules. Reaching on time, doing the assigned work and getting salary — are these all that the employees and the management expect from each other? With time, the roles and expectations of management and employees have also been redefined. The management is increasingly aware that a motivated employee is an asset. An employee is also an ambassador of goodwill. If the relationships are suffocating within an organisation, they inevitably have their echo externally. Who should communicate to the employees? The answer is, both personnel and Public Relations, each having its area defined. While information relating to policies, procedures, welfare activities and trade union negotiations clearly come under the purview of personnel, creating avenues and channels for employees expression, motivation and indoctrination are clearly Public Relations functions.

Law

In times of crisis, specially in cases of alleged libel or slander, top management seeks legal aid to get out of the mess. In such times, it generally refuses to speak to the media because the counsel may have advised them to keep quiet. Ivy Lee felt very strongly about this. "I have seen more situations where the public ought to understand, and where the public would sympathise with", he remarked, "spoiled by the intervention of the lawyer than in any other way. Whenever a lawyer starts to talk to the public, he shuts out the light". Close cooperation between public relations and law is the requirement of the time as the issues are growing complex. Safety, environment, health and resettlement are some of the issues which occupy the minds of the corporate managers. With increasing expectation and awareness among the employees, the specialist groups and the lobbies, public relations may have to respond to their queries through media intervention. While dealing with the issues in print and through other channels of communication, it is very necessary that while taking care of the legal aspects, the human touch is not lost in communication.

Finance

Besides the shareholders, the financial community, stock exchanges and the financial press form important "publics" for the public relations department. The requirements of all these publics are specific, hence the communication packages designed for them should have the expertise of the finance department and the language and presentation skills of the public relations department. The finance department must also be made aware of the value and objectives of Public Relations activities. Expenditure on Public Relations, advertising and publicity is still considered by many finance experts as dispensable. When there is a financial crunch, the victims more often then not are the Public Relations and advertising departments. The finance officers are trained budget slashers.

Production

Public relations has to speak about the product and the organisation. In order to write stories in the employees' house journal and communicate through other channels, it is imperative for a Public relations person to go to the factories and shopfloors and see the way a product is processed, assembled and produced. He should see the human effort involved, the drama, the risks, the fun, almost everything. The raw materials for Public Relations are the real life happenings. The Public Relations person must visualise what would be interesting news to which public and how to give things a human angle. He should also highlight the marvels of the human spirit against odds. The Public Relations person has to be motivated himself before he can motivate and influence others. Besides knowing the product attributes of his organisation, he must gather data about the competitors' products and activities. Nothing goes waste. In fact there is no substitute for knowledge, which a Public Relations person must understand. For motivating employees in the production line, Public Relations can play a complementary role to the production chief by working out incentives, covering human interest features, giving news about the employees who excel in meeting targets or prove innovative on the production floor.

A continuous dialogue with the chief of the production will give enough material for making the internal media interesting and employees oriented.

Controlling Rift and Synergise

The committee should meet periodically say once a week or a fortnight and discuss areas where Public Relations could be put to use. The Public Relations manager can bring proposals, discuss the thrust areas and work out programmes aimed at different publics. Sub-delegation or attendance by proxy should be discouraged. The chief executive officer (CEO) should also once in a while be invited to participate in the deliberations to land more weight and seriousness to the discussions. The annual programme both at the macro and micro levels should ideally be presented through a written proposal accompanied by slides, charts and pilot films to the Board of Directors not only to make the top management aware of the thrust areas but to make them appreciate the role and dimensions of public relations.

2

Public Relations: Functions and Scope

Basically, with the expansion of public relations activities to different types of organisations, the nature of its functions have also undergone change. Twenty years ago, no public relations practitioner would have agreed that communicating with its employees is one of the functions of public relations department but hardly any practitioner and professional today can deny that it is a public relations function.

The concept prevalent at that time was that any public relations department should organise a Press conference at the time of launching of new company, new product, new service and new financial year with highlights of the achievements of previous financial year, issue clarification on any controversy regarding company in newspapers, manage press coverage of company's activities from time to time, lobby among Government circles to obtain licences at the cost of competitors and do liaison work with various Government departments to procure faster electricity connections, telephone lines, release of quotas of raw materials etc.

Briefly, public relations practitioners were looked upon as the Ali Baba of the Company' who should solve all critical problems as and when it is confronted by them. The emphasis was on 'Management by Drive' rather than 'Management by Objectives' (MbO).

Consequently, public relations was not conceived by most of the organisations as an continuous ongoing function, but as an intermittent function.

To attend to this intermittent functions, organisations used to employ 'Supermen' who used to be either children of senior government officials or had direct relations with those working in positions where from they could extend favours to the company as and when required. It was only after exhausting such channels, that the company started appointing people who had contacts but no relations with concerned officials.

The changes in the functions performed by public relations department along with other reasons are also attributed to the changes in the type of people who are employed or appointed in department. Their attitude, philosophy, and motivational profile not only towards their own profession but also towards life in general has a direct bearing on the functions they perform. The other factors responsible for change in functions are the attitude and support of top management, degree of professionalisation prevalent in the company, in the public relations department and its other departments, marketing conditions such as competition, market share, location of customers etc.

1. Traditional Functions

The public relations functions are a continuous and ongoing process, apart from being dynamic. Defining the function of public relations, one can say that it is a method of bringing the desired public acceptance, good will and understanding among various publics about the company's policies, procedures and products. But how it is done by companies, is very difficult if not impossible to explain as no two organisations adopt the same method or combination of different methods to produce identical results. With the passage of time the objectives of these functions and their methods have changed as well as drastically changed the means utilised for this purpose have undergone vast changes.

Press conference, social advertising, propaganda meeting, distribution of handbills etc., are the tools of public relations. They are only the means to achieve public relations objectives. Application of these tools or means to achieve Public Relations objectives is the function of public relations department. If a company decides to organise "free servicing of its product" for a week with an objective to improve its relations and understanding with the existing customers, the public relations function is to tie up with various dealers, arrange for the services of its service personnel at the dealers premises, collection of feedback from customers regarding the quality of product and the types of problems commonly faced by them, educating them about company's policy, usage of product etc., and for informing the customers about its campaign, it may give advertisement in the newspapers and the electronic media, put up hoardings, distribute handbills which will be the means to inform public and it does not become public relations functions.

For performing such an activity public relations department seeks the help and assistance of the concerned department which in this case would be the marketing department of the company. Therefore, the function of public relations department would be conceptualising the innovative methods to reach out to various publics to gain their acceptance, awareness and ultimately their good will in order to ensure their continued support and patronage for fulfilling its business objectives, proper support from top management, smooth implementation of the project and to give feedback to the top management and the concerned department to further improve its activities on the basis of marked research and data collection undertaken during project implementation. The traditional functions of public relations were based on the objective 'to increase the profitability of the company', but the modern functions take a much wider perspective of public relations as a management function, business, profession or vocation whereby company foresees a much wider role for itself to improve the quality of life of publics at large rather than confining itself only to 'profit motive'.

In the context of contents of the functions, public opinion and communication were two major functions of public relations department in the past. The major emphasis was on building public opinion on the basis of propaganda at special occasions rather than on the basis of educating public, primarily because companies wanted quick returns out of investment in the public relations department.

In communication functions also, the concentration was on communicating with external publics such as customers, dealers, suppliers, financiers, shareholders, Government agencies, press and various influence groups. Among the influence groups, various religious groups and political parties were predominant, being the major public opinion holders for which the general public cared at lot. Communication with employees was considered non-consequential because they were not looked upon more than a means of production and for them money was considered as the only motivator.

The poor bargaining power, availability of large manpower chasing too few jobs and lack of trade union movement were some of the factors for apathy of the management and owners towards their employees as a result of which they never considered it prudent to care communicating with them. It was towards the end of World War II, when the need for skilled manpower was suddenly realised by most of the companies and they found that without favourable employees opinion, it was very difficult for them to survive in business. It was then the public relations practitioners were asked by their top managements to address themselves to this live problem of the industry. Today, communication with employees is considered as the most essential function of the public relations practitioners in absence of which communication with various external publics is likely to have little effect.

A motivated and prosperous work-force acts as the ambassador of the company and creates everlasting positive opinion among the external publics about the company, its philosophy, values, politics, procedures, products and services etc.

Modern Functions of Public Relations

The new set of functions of public relations department is emerging out of changes in values, philosophies and attitude of the top management of most of the organisations. They do not look at Public Relations as a quick cause-and-effect syndrome anymore. In order to be effective, public relations has to be thought of as a long-term strategy and to implement this long-term strategy in a phased manner, appropriate short-term strategies are to be evolved and implemented to build up and maintain the tempo.

1. *Evaluation:* In the increasingly competitive world of today, no company would like to invest their funds and other resources on undertaking any public relations programme without ensuring for itself the likely gains to the organisation or whether their programmes are viewed by the public in the same perspective with which they are

designed. The increasing risk of failure and the high cost of programmes have made it essential to evaluate the programmes from time to time not only to ensure achievement of its objectives but also to increase the intensity of their impact. The evaluation of programmes is no more looked upon as an adhoc activity but it is undertaken on a continuous basis even during the implementation of the programme itself so that if there is a need to change the strategy in between, it could be done without causing much loss. Evaluation of programmes relating to building of corporate image, social advertising, building of favourable customer attitudes towards company and building up of sympathetic attitude among publics whose favour is essential for survival and growth of business, is normally undertaken by public relations department.

These evaluations are done during the course of the above campaigns as well as on their completion, primarily to ensure that these campaigns could be flexible to adopt to the changes in the environment. Unlike other business plans where the environment is relatively stable, one of the essential peculiarities of public relations functions is that one deals with human beings who are live and vibrant which makes the environment highly unstable and unpredictable.

2. *Research:* Research starts before understanding a particular function to study the problem in great details in order to establish real or the core problem. Apart from it, it also helps to give more objective an outlook to the problem as it turns out to be no more based on the perception of just a few people. Research has made Public Relations a broad-based function and enhanced its credibility. Investigative journalism based on the data collected from affected people and market research before launching a new product or testing its success are the two major

contributions of research while attitude surveys and opinion polls are some other advantages.

The preparations or the changes in the personnel policies of many organisations are undertaken based on the feedback from the attitude survey undertaken among employees from time to time. Similarly market research surveys undertaken based on the feedback from the attitude surveys by consultancy organisations from time to time show the relative rating of the companies on various aspects such as market leadership, social contribution, fair policies, concern for consumer etc., which compel the concerned companies to have a fresh look at their policies, strategies, methods and priorities and the need for improvement in the respective areas. The application of public relations research has been so widely accepted in various aspects of our life that even for forecasting the performance of various political parties in the General Elections, it is not uncommon these days that you see general public in bazars, playgrounds and offices quoting extensively from the findings of such researches.

3. *Counselling:* In fact the emergence of counselling function itself has grown arising out of increasing concern for various publics and to develop lasting relationships with them. How is this function different from the traditional function of having a dialogue with various publics can be understood from the difference of objectives in both the cases.

When the public relations officer of a company used to interact with customers earlier, the basic purpose was to give them a feeling that company wants to listen to their problems, but today the objective is to have an in-depth study of the issue by understanding the basic grievances of the customers, exchange important information about the company, inviting their suggestions to resolve these grievances and explain why some of suggestions given by them are not feasible to be implemented.

The crux of the issue is to develop a lasting relationship with them, giving them their legitimate share of, say about the company, its policies and products due to be developed, based on the feedback received from customers or any publics with which public relations department is interacting. The approach of counselling needs lot of time, money and resources on behalf of the company as well as public relations department, but the results achieved are equally satisfying and rewarding. The understanding required on the part of public relations practitioners and professionals is of much higher order in this case as they have to have sound knowledge of human psychology, behavioural science and interpersonal skills. It is a very effective method of developing relationship, understanding and trust with various publics, but if not used properly it could prove dangerous and defeat the very purpose of undertaking this exercise. It needs a series of meeting between the parties over a period of a time at different occasions to give better understanding and opportunities of each other. It is the quality of interaction rather than the quantity of interaction with publics which is the underlying principle of counselling.

The communication developed through counselling between public relations department and the concerned public is more open with least apprehensions and doubts in the minds of the parties where both are equally sharing the information and through a free frank discussion. The first step in counselling session is physical arrangement of the place where both the parties are meeting. It should be such that you are able to give your complete and undivided attention to the party so as to enable you to listen to them attentively. During the second step, the concerned public starts narrating its problems without disclosing the details and if it finds in public relations professional a good and attentive listener it may go to the next stage. Once the details of the problem are shared between the parties with open mind to resolve the problem, it is not difficult to find the core problem. The Public Relations professional should be sensitive to the feelings and needs of the public which helps to discover and explore the possible solutions. An important aspect of successful counselling is avoidance of criticism. These criticisms may have place in communication but in a counselling session, as a rule, one should be careful to avoid it.

Joint explanation helps in working out various alternative solutions and the alternate which will give the optimum result can be mutually arrived out and implemented to generate good will and understanding. If the alternate has to be implemented by the public, the discussion could be concluded at the stage of arriving at the optimum alternate because helping the client or the public to help themselves is another golden principle of professional counselling.

Public Relations Consultants

Comparatively, Public relations consultancy in India is recent phenomenon which came into existence barely a few years ago. Within a short span it has made fast strides due to overwhelming response from not only established industrial houses but also from comparatively smaller and new companies. Although the most of the business of public relations consultancy in our country is run by advertising agencies which do not claim any expertise in public relations functions, yet they continue with it purely from business and convenience point of view because they do possess expertise in the allied functions of public relations. The lack of independent public relations consultancy network is greatly responsible for this kind of situation.

However, now the situation is fast changing as more and more companies are facing peculiar public relations problems which demand high level of professional inputs which these advertising agencies normally lack. This has given birth to exclusive public relations consultancy outfits or management consultancy firms who provide specialised services in Public Relations along with marketing, personnel etc. But these firms are concentrated in metro cities only as the business opportunities are available there alone. In due course of time, they may spread out all over the country as the concept gains popularity. In Mumbai, we have public relations consultancy companies like Good Reforms, Channel Plus, Dutta & Dutta etc. In Delhi too, public relation professionals like Ajit S. Gopal, Anil Basu, and many more have opened their own consultancy outfits and their number is increasing with the growing awareness among industries about the importance of public relations. What kind of companies avail the services of these consultants? Let us discuss as what are their intrinsic advantages vis-a-vis company's own public relations department and what are the functions which are best suited to the company to involve them.

Types of Companies

Esssentially, all companies need the help of public relations consultants at one time or another. While for small companies, it is very difficult to get professionals for establishing its own public relations department with right type of educational qualifications and experience, apart from being expensive; for large companies it is the problem of objectivity and vested interests within the company which compels it to take, the help of public relations consultants.

The reasons for engaging consultants may differ from company to company but their contribution and effectiveness can hardly be questioned keeping in mind their objectivity, vast pool of knowledge, analytical ability and capability to produce results in short time even in critical situations. A majority of Public Relations consultancy firms offer a full range of services, from news releases to special events, but some specialise in graphics or financial affairs or influencing the pressure or interest groups. Although advertising agencies were initially reluctant to incorporate the public relations functions, but now big advertising agencies like Hindustan Thompson Associates, Lintas, Trikaya Grey, Mudra etc., have done suitable restructuring in their respective organisations to provide Public Relations consultancy services.

Selection of Public Relations Consultants

Although it is extremely difficult to generalise any formula for picking up public relations consultants yet some major guidelines will prove quite useful for a company to concretise its thinking on the issue and select an appropriate consultant.

(a) *Clients*—existing clients list past clients, average number of clients during last three years, retainership clients, project clients, old clients and number of years of association, average length of relationship with clients, clients lost in last year.

(b) *Competence and reputation*—years in business, size, people, and billing full services (specialities), reach (local, regional, national, international); growth pattern, financial stability, types of accounts, experience of similar accounts, samples of work, sample list of suppliers.

(c) *Results and measurement*—does the firm understand your-objectives/needs; how the progress will be reported; how results will be measured; what will be cost of billing, how rate expenses will be billed, approval process etc.

(d) *Staff*—list and qualifications of staff (full time, freelance, consultants); staff to be assigned for one's assignment—qualifications and service with firms, percentage of their time to be devoted to your assignment; secretarial and backup staff available, staff turnover in last two years.

Once one has have finalised his decision, one may collect some additional information about the firm from its previous clients, its previous employees, its credit worthiness and the reputation enjoyed by it at professional forums and among media people. These may not ensure the selection of best consultants by itself, but will definitely reduce the chances of picking up a rough consultant or the possibility of differences with him at a later date.

Assignments Nature

Infact, what type of assignments are performed by these Public Relations consultancy firms, depends on a variety of factors such as needs of the business organisation, the skills and competence of the personnel working in the Public Relations department of the company, urgency of assignment, objectivity of the assignment and the type of work culture prevailing in the company etc. In most of the public sector undertakings in our country, the apparent justification given for engaging a Public Relations consultant, is the volume of assignments already handled by the Public Relations department or off-shoot of some events like visit by the parliamentary committee, preparations of annual report, designing manuals or translation of documents from Hindi to English or vice versa etc. In private sector, the Public Relations consultants are primarily engaged due to absence of in-house Public Relations department or lack of appropriate expertise and skills, urgency of assignment; or the quality of work primarily designed for a specific public, pressure group, press etc.

The basic function, of a Public Relations consultancy firm is to provide tailor-made services depending on the needs of the customer/client but many a time a company is not even aware of its needs or objectives and yet appoints a Public Relations consultant to provide overall Public Relations services to the company. In such a situation, the consultancy firm measures his client by conducting a systematic study of the client's organisation, policies, strengths and weaknesses, competitive position, needs, problems and work culture. The account team responsible for handling the client then gets to work setting objectives and goals and developing an overall public relations plan and budget to implement it. Some large consultancy firms get the plan and budget approved by a team of their senior colleagues before submitting it for approval of the client. Once the client approves the programme, the account team puts it into effect utilising the members of the team, senior management and specialized department of the consultant's firm. The types of assignment can be broadly divided into two categories i.e. project assignment such as writing releases, handling press conference and media contact, conducting opinion surveys, research on specific problems and general studies, handling Annual General meeting and special events like exhibition etc., writing and preparing publications and brochures and similar tasks which are essentially one-time exercises. The other type of assignment is normally known as retainership assignment which continues for an indefinite period dealing with total public relations function or establishing public relations department and running it for such time till the in-house employees become fully confident and competent to handle it themselves.

The payment to a consultancy firm is also governed by the type of assignment handled by it. Normally any of the following four methods may be adopted for fixation and payment of fee of the consultants:

Notably consultant to give the assignment to the person who can do proper justice to it Similarly a consultant should also not accept an assignment which he cannot fulfil within the given time-frame and to the satisfaction of the customer company. In order to avoid the possible areas of difference of opinion or misunderstanding, the following course of action is suggested for the consultant:

(a) Avoid confrontation with the company and its personnel even if they are not cooperating. Adopt advisory and counselling approach to get the optimum result from the situation. Always remember that consultant does not have any direct power in the hierarchy of the company irrespective of his enjoying confidence of certain key personnel in the company. His most important power is his 'knowledge and his most effective tool is 'persuasion and counselling'.

(b) Do the job as meticulously as possible to earn the client's good will and confidence.

(c) Keep accurate time sheet with details of accomplishment on a day-to-day basis with details of any impending problems restricting the performance of consultant. Any support or information supposed to be provided by the company should be brought to its notice on a daily basis, preferably in writing to avoid misunderstanding at a later date.

(d) Develop a clear understanding of the client company's problem/assignment before accepting it and keep the company informed from time to time about the progress of the work so as to develop mutual understanding and trust.

(e) Differences in the work style of employees are quite natural as the personalities. Therefore as long as they are on the right track, they should not be disturbed.

(f) Adherence to professional ethics and taking an impartial and independent approach to the problems, may create sometimes temporary setbacks for the consultant. It should not deter him from doing so because in the long run his higher credibility and professional approach will compensate the inconvenience which he might have faced initially.

(g) Avoid feedback until and unless it is specifically sought by someone in the company. While giving feedback about the diagnosis, analysis and the possible solution, the consultant should be factual rather than judgemental.

Advantages

Much against the normal perception that it is only small or medium size company who need the consultant most, even the big multinationals are also availing of their services frequently. It is needless here to emphasize that it is over and above their own public relations department. What are the reasons and advantages of engaging a Public Relations consultant can be summarised as under.

1. The multi-company and multi-work culture *experience* is of immense value to the company by which they get to know the practices prevailing in other companies.
2. The one big advantage of engaging a consultant is his highly *specialised knowledge,* complete with multicompany exposure, making him intelligent, mature and a receptive person who could be relied upon by company in difficult times.
3. As and when the company has any specific problem, it can immediately contact the Public Relations consultant for his *expert advice.*
4. Consultant is most *cost effective for* the company as company pays him as long as it needs him. Moreover there is no permanent liability of consultant as in case of employees. The cost incurred by company on a consultant is directly related to the quality and quantity of work.
5. The *convenience* of getting the consultant as and when the need arises, is one of the best advantages for the company. It reduces their business risk and the fear of unknown situations.
6. Consultant being an outsider is not restricted by the hierarchy of the organisation in performance of his duties and mostly gives attention at the topmost level of the organisation. Being an outsider, his *advice is objective, unbiased, creative and innovative* and not restricted or limited due to various impediments in the work culture of the organisation.
7. As an expert in the profession, a consultant adopts supportive and collaborative approach towards the company's employees in the analysis, implementation and review of the programmes undertaken by him. Most often the positive and

creative suggestions given by the employees are ignored by the company in its day to day functioning.

8. The consultant takes as a visionary long-term perspective of the problems, in resolving them. His role is not only confined to the resolution of existing problems of the company but also to mark the future course of action. He broadens vision of the management and employees by virtue of his experience of other organisations. The persuasive and counselling approach taken by him helps in softening the attitudes of the employees and in his flexible approach.

Departmental Functions

If the Public Relations functions are considered important in the company by the top management it may create a publicity section. Advertising section, news/ information section, graphic/photo section and grievance section etc., but if it is not considered important by the top management it may be assigned some odd jobs like transportation, guest house, liaison etc. Mostly the publicity section looks after preparation of publicity material, its implementation and review from time to time of its publicity strategies to create the desired impact on the publics. It is responsible for show rooms, trade fairs, exhibitions, hand bills, and contests among publics. The work of the advertising section is to decide the advertising strategies and budget in consultation with Marketing Department, design advertising campaigns, liaison with advertising agencies, study the response of various advertisements in print and electronic media, message and their content.

Again News/Information desk is responsible for press coverage, keeping the records of press clippings on subjects of interest to the company, passing on such clippings to the concerned officials, imparting information about the company's performance and stand on various issues to the press, holding press conferences, press releases issue.

Whereas Graphic/photo/layout section develops and designs the visual part of the publicity material brochures/ information bulletins and house journal of the company while the editorial cell of this section develops the written material including its editing. It is this section which is responsible for designing and developing various types of literature for the company such as house journal, special journal for customers, distributors, suppliers, shareholders, Annual reports, special messages for employees, shareholders for subscribing to rights issue etc. Grievance section constantly interacts with various publics who are unable to get their grievances resolved from the concerned department of the company in the first instance. In many companies in India, the public relations department is directly made incharge of enquiries and grievance redressal and members of concerned public do not have to interact with any other department.

This arrangement on one side ensures that members of public are attended to by fully trained and competent staff of public relations department while on the other side they save the employees of other departments of their valuable time. It entertains complaints and grievances from customers, investors, shareholders, suppliers, distributors, press and electronic media, financial institutions, governmental agencies, community and various special interest groups.

Integration of Public Relations Department and Consultant's Functions

To what extent company performs Public Relations

functions itself and to what extent it uses the services of a consultant is determined by the number, size and importance of the publics involved; the attitudes of the publics towards the company; the size and financial resources of the company; the size, competence and exposure of its public relations department and the social, political, economic and technological climate in which the company is operating. One most convenient situation where most companies decide to engage the services of the Public Relations consultant is when suddenly there is an increase in the volume of work of public relations department for a temporary period. Such situations could arise during modernisation and expansion of the company's business activities or during its involvement in some controversy, take over bid by competitor, infighting among the family controlling the business enterprise. The visit by various Committees of Parliament members in a Public Sector undertaking is another such occasion for engaging the services of Public Relations consultant, often on exhorbitent fee.

Another prominent reason of contracting out assignments to consultants may be due to Public Sector undertaking's poor productivity of the available manpower and lack of managerial skill to get the work done from existing employees. On the other hand, in most of the private sector companies, the tendency on the part of management is to get the consultant at as cheap a fee as possible. The law of diminishing returns seems to be applicable in such a situation where a consultant may not refuse the assignment keeping in mind his long-term interest but due to poor fee, his motivation and interest in the assignment can be easily visualised.

Though a company cannot depend on consultants forever to run its public relations activities, it has to avail of their services for a variety of reasons such as objectivity of feedback, expertise, degree of competence, their knowledge of practices of competitors and the changes taking place in the business environment outside. Even in those companies where Public Relations employees do not lack in competence or expertise, the presence of Public Relations consultant puts them on their guard by providing competition and motivating them to come out with their best.

Scope

Gradually, the scope and the nature of public relations functions is going to be wider and wider with the growing environment becomes more and more complex and competitive. There is a growing awareness among customers, employees, press and other publics about the responsibilities of the company towards them and as a result of which they are becoming more and more demanding. The success of business enterprises in future will greatly depend on the channels of communication they maintain with different publics and the resultant opinion of these publics about their products or services.

Many existing functions will lose lustre and importance and many new functions will emerge on the horizon of the public relations. Instead of one annual general meeting with its shareholders, a company may have to have many meetings with them to enjoy their continued support for the growth and development of business because a most effective project may not take off if it is not properly communicated to shareholders and the investing and other publics at large. The current form of advertising may not last for more than a few years as it fails to educate the customers and is no different from publicity. The emphasis will have to shift from artificial issues to real ones such as product superiority, price and range, availability to customers in different parts of the country etc. Press relations cannot continue to be only an annual feature around the annual general meeting of the company but have to be much more interactive and understanding. The role of press will itself be taken over by the electronic media specially when most of the established newspaper groups in our country have come out with video magazines which are less time consuming and are live, entertaining and do not require a very high degree of concentration.

Summing Up

It is observed that more and more companies, big or small, are organising and reorganising their public relations departments now. In doing so, they are taking the help of outside consultants to share their expertise, competence and experience for the advantage of the company. The new functions which are increasing by the day and given importance by many organisations include research, evaluation and counselling. Traditional functions of public relations being publicity, advertising, news/information and magazine publication, designing graphics, photographs, attending to the grievances from various publics and their effective redressal also form part of its charge.

REFERENCES

1. *Public Relations Practices, Case studies*, Englewood Cliffs N.J., Prentice-Hall, 1975.
2. Norman (1952), *Public Relations,* University of Oklahoma Press.
3. *Undertaking Public Relations,* New York; Lord Products, 1963.

3

Law and Ethics of Public Relations

Generally as a convention it is seen that every profession also has a code of ethics. The code of ethics becomes the governing principle for the practitioners of these trades. If they cross that, they could find themselves in professional, ethical or personal dilemma.

Basically, 'Public relations' is the art and science of relating to the publics. Communication is its nervous system. If there is no communication, there is no PR. The profession demands of public relations practitioners to Write, Write and Write a lot for varying publics such as employees, shareholders, legislators, bureaucrats, consumers, the media and the people at large. Even a routine job like issuing a press release, preparing a performance report or editing a house journal could prove challenging from the legal and ethical points of view, if the PR person is not careful. Hence he must have a basic knowledge of the law governing the profession and the professional code of ethics.

According to Dennis L. Wilcox and others, (*Public Relations Writings and Media Techniques*), "Public relations writing is supposed to produce favourable results, but if the writer is careless, there may be adverse reactions ranging from hurt feelings to suits for damages."

Here is given some of the laws and ethical aspects governing the profession of Public Relations.

Libel: Any false statement about a person printed or broadcast and which brings upon this person hatred, contempt or inflicts injury or mental torture or has an adverse effect on his occupation or business constitutes libel. If it is made by a person verbally, it amounts to slander. There have been many cases in the recent past when public figures — celebrities, politicians and bureaucrats — have sued newspapers and magazines for libel claiming a fortune as damages. Since most of the public relations work is planned to create a favourable impression about an organisation or person, normally there should be no difficulty in avoiding libel. In political campaigns, however, such situations do occur, hence it is advisable to get the documents or messages legally vetted. Pictures or visuals can equally be libellous. A picture in a national newspaper showing mules outside Parliament House was treated by some parliamentarians as derogatory and a breach of their privilege some time ago. Similarly, pictures showing the President of India stumbling at a public function were considered in bad taste, though not libellous. Most libel cases happen because either the news source or the reporter becomes careless. Libel, however, has three defences, viz., truth, fair comment, criticism and privilege. If the writer can prove what he has written is true with documentary evidence, he can fight a libel suit.

Slander: Slander is much like libel except that instead of being written, it is spoken. It can occur in a broadcast, in a speech or in an informal conversation. In any case, it must be heard by a third party. If a person is called a liar or a thief, it is not a slander if no one is present. If anyone else hears, it becomes slander. The safeguard against it is to avoid saying anything detrimental to anyone. One may be considered a cheat or a crook or some organisation may be fraudulent, but unless you have the backing of a court judgment saying so, the PR person is best advised to avoid it.

Parliamentarians in India enjoy the privilege of immunity if they utter or say anything against opponents or others within the precincts of the House. Reporting such comment also enjoys immunity from legal action provided it is accurate.

Privacy Invasion

As a recent development we come across the fact that, there has been an increase in sensitivity to invasion of privacy in recent times. In general, law and law suits strive to prevent anyone from knowing anything about an individual which the person concerned does not want to be known.

When an advertiser wants to use a person's name or picture, a is necessary to secure his written consent on that document which clearly defines the intended use. In the area of privacy, the practitioners in charge of hospital public information have to be careful. The privacy of patients and their medical records must be preserved. For an interview with a photograph of a patient, prior permission must be obtained. Similarly in case of medico-legal cases, the request to interview or photograph a patient under arrest or custody must be referred to the police department and other concerned government agencies. In giving a statement about the condition of a patient, the hospital spokesperson should never offer a prognosis. In the case of the death of a prominent person, the hospital has the responsibility to inform the next of kin before contacting the press. The coverage of AIDS presents a difficult ethical problem confronting the media. The syndrome has aroused acute public interest, thereby making the patient the subject of social curiosity. When the victim is a celebrity or an important person, the curiosity is intensified. Under what conditions should the names of the victims be identified to the media is an important question which must be dealt with carefully.

Copyright

The copyright law applies not only to written words but to illustrations, plays, musical works, motion pictures, sound recordings, graphics, sculptures, pantomimes and dances. The aim of a copyright is to secure for the creator of the material all the benefits accruing from its creation. The Copyright Act grants the copyright holder the exclusive right to print, publish, or reproduce an original literary, musical, or artistic work for a certain number of years. The law provides exclusive right for hire of the creator and 50 years beyond for those who own the copyright.

Public relations practitioners should be careful not to reproduce material in their publications beyond the limit set by the Copyright Act. It is remarkable here to note that fair use for purposes of criticism, comment, news reporting, teaching, scholarship, or research does not amount to infringement. Similarly, article reprints also require written permission.

Remember Ignorance of the law does not provide protection to the offender. Hence it is in the interest of the public relations practitioners to keep copies of all the acts concerning the above and other laws governing the press, trade marks, contempt of court. National Security Act, Criminal Procedure Code etc. for ready reference with them.

Guiding Ethics

A Public Relation practitioner's conduct must go beyond mere avoidance of legal ramifications. The work according to Wilcox Nolte "should be honest and honorable. It should be fair and reasonable. It should stay far away from flattery".

According to Lovell ethics is governed by two factors: the code of professional standards, and the conscience and training of PR people themselves.

The "Code of Athens" adopted by the International Public Relations Association in Athens in 1965 has been adopted by member countries including the Public Relations Society of India. The code expects the following from the practitioners:

Every member of IPRA must endeavour.

1. To encourage the creation of patterns and networks of communication which, in sponsoring the free circulation of essential information, would enable everyone within the group to feel informed, concerned, responsible and part of a team.
2. To contribute towards the realisation of those moral and cultural conditions which will enable man to enjoy the inalienable rights which are recognised as his in the 'Universal Declaration of the Rights of Man'. (United Nations, 10 December 1948).
3. To behave on all occasions and in all circumstances in such a way as to deserve the confidence of all those with whom they come into contact.
4. To take into account the fact that because of the public character of his profession, his behaviour, even in private, he will have an effect upon the judgements formed about the profession as a whole.

Every member must undertake:

5. To respect, in the excercise of his profession, the moral principles and rules of the 'Universal Declaration of the Rights of Man'.

6. To respect and uphold the dignity of the human person and recognise that each individual has the right to form, by himself, his own judgement.
7. To create the moral, psychological and intellectual conditions of the true interchange of ideas, to recognise the right of the parties involved to explain their cases and express their points of view.
8. To respect his promise and engagements, which must always be arranged in terms which do not lead to confusion, and act honestly and loyally on every occasion in order to safeguard the confidence of both present and former clients or employers.
9. To act, in all circumstances, in such a way as to take due note of the respective interests of the parties concerned, by constantly establishing the relationship between, on the one hand, the neeeds and wishes of the public concerned, and, on the other hand, those of the organisation.

Every member must undertake not:

10. To subordinate truth to other considerations.
11. To disseminate information not based upon checked facts or tacts that can be checked.
12. To lend his assistance to any enterprise or action which might harm the moral honesty, dignity or integrity of the human person.
13. To make use of any method or technique which will tend to influence the subconscious mind of individuals in order to make them act irrationally and, by so doing, free them from the responsibility of their actions.

Amazingly, opinions about the ethical and moral values of public relations people vary widely. Donald K. Wright

(*Ethics in Public Relations*) says that when we speak of ethics in public relations, we usually speak of lack of ethics. Can ethical values be measured? Scales with the greatest validity according to Wright are those designed to measure individual moral and ethical values. PR people have their own viewpoints on ethics, evolved with years of experience.

It is apt here to quote Joan Dolph,"The professional people who have lasted are as ethical as in any other profession," "It is just good business. You have to have a token for everything that is offered. A good newsperson is as interested in a good story as you are. If they respect you and you respect them, you do not have to be unethical in your dealing with them."

The carrying capability of several thousand voice conversation, or TV pictures, or computer streams of information over long distances is the coming thing. These technologies, complemented by innovations in printing technology, colour reproduction, use of computer graphics, desktop publishing, and use of computers for research have given tremendous opportunities to the public relations practitioners.

Again the question arises can mass communication be a substitute for interpersonal communication and folk media, especially in the context of Indian society? The answer to this is, both have to complement each other. With a spurt in technology on the one hand, and the multifarious challenges, it is increasingly felt that a modern organisation can no longer use the tools in isolation from different forces at work. Advertising, public relations, promotion, information, market research, direct and indirect marketing, rural media and now tele-marketing all need integrated communication. The main aim is reaching out to different publics for selling a product, a service or an idea. All need a climate of understanding and human approach.

To quote, Sanat Lahiri, "we must be public relations humanists. For the goal of public relations is to reach and touch the hearts and minds of men and women". With the world turning into a virtual cauldron of simmering problems, societies, nations need a humane approach.

4

Management of Public Relations

A modern organisation is considered as a living entity. The organic approach to management recognises that the health of an individual department or "organ" will influence the general health of the whole organisation. Profit is the bottomline and is no doubt the life-blood of the organisation. But equally, the communication system is its nervous system.

The following are the major communication tasks in an organisation.

1. Processing environment is one of the very important functions of an organisation. The information gathered facilitates goal-setting and decision-making about various aspects like production attributes, diversification, and strategic planning. Keeping a vigil on competitor's activities and products is an important aspect of market surveillance. All the information thus gathered is studied, sifted, processed and made to percolate to different internal departments. Primarily getting information from the environment is a communication activity.

2. The second stage is to identify the outside "publics" and accommodate information in the communication messages designed for various publics. To illustrate, the private airlines recently introduced in our country the need to communicate to their potential publics/clients that they offer safe, reliable and economical air

transportation. To do this, each organisation must advertise, provide free trial service to some, encourage employees to be polite and so forth. Different communication techniques are required vis-a-vis different publics. There can also be a situation where an organisation has just one client and still it cannot do without communication.

3. Within an organisation, it is necessary to establish the attitudinal environment of the communication situation. Supervision is the task of a few members of an organisation. Interpersonal communication is required to achieve the goals of the department. In any given organisation, we never have a situation when everyone is satisfied. Some are unhappy for various reasons. Among other reasons, some experience job dissatisfaction. This situation could arise due to two reasons. Firstly the employee may think that he does not have enough information to do the job. Second, interpersonal relations among the unit's members may be poor. Job satisfaction is a very complex area. People enjoy or dislike their job for various reasons which should be removed.

Maybe some employees have the supervisory role of controlling others as part of the hierarchical system within an organisation. Such people are referred to as managers or leaders. Communication in the organisational context involves an attempt by the leader to establish open relationships with subordinates. This helps the leader receive and transmit information effective managerial communication however, is often subjective.

Communication after all is intrinsic to all kinds of jobs like production, processing, packaging or marketing, so how does Public Relations specifically contribute to organisational communication? The answer is that communication is not the business of the public relations department alone. Public relations is the process through which an environment can be created for effective communication.

Most often public relations is referred to as a top management function. The responsibility of communicating with different publics ultimately rests with the top management. Public Relations shows how to go about the act of communication. It helps decide what to communicate, to whom and through which channel or channels.

Public relations is a link between the management and its various politics of all the forms of communication, interpersonal communication probably is the best. It is also referred to as face to face communication. Organisations at times are very large, multi-locational, multi-directional conglomerates, employing millions of employees speaking different languages having different specialisations. Hence it is imperative to create the right channels to reach out to the varied constituent publics. It is the responsibility of the public relations department to understand the communication requirements of these publics, select channels and prepare relevant communication packages and evaluate their efficacy and impact frequently.

Notably, media relations can be both proactive and reactive. By the former it is meant that a Public Relations practitioner plans to get his organisation's news covered by the media as a planned effort. At other times, he may have to react to certain press coverage which the organisation feels is not based on facts and has earned negative publicity in the minds of the readers. React he must, but not till he is fully convinced that the story is malicious or derogatory or unflattering to his company. Also when he reacts, he should have facts and data to back up his organisation's point of view. In this situation, he may have to issue a rejoinder clarifying management's point of view or meet the concerned correspondent or news editor, depending on the extent of damage caused due to irresponsible reporting.

MEDIA OF PUBLIC RELATIONS

1. Television: The advent of television has been a watershed in the world of communication. A force to reckon with, television has a great scope as a publicity medium. A medium which allows the use of the printed word, the spoken word, pictures in motion, colour, music, animation, and sound effects, all blended in one message. With satellite communication becoming a reality, the powerful, pervasive impact of TV is worldwide. Being an intimate mass medium, TV has great communication potential for a Public Relations person. There are certain ground rules which, if followed, can get enormous publicity for an organisation through this medium. The starting point is to understand the working of various TV channels available and their programme content, and then to decide dispassionately what aspect of our company is newsworthy. As TV is a visual medium, the subject has to be colourful and action-oriented. A dull meeting, a panel discussion or a laboratory discovery are not subjects for making TV news releases. A news release will not be accepted if it is too sales oriented or looks and sounds like a commercial. The best approach is to make an informational clip which has news value for the viewer. The name of the organisation should appear incidentally. Non-profit organisations stand a better chance of getting coverage for their activities due to the nature of their work.

A news release should not exceed 90 seconds. The story should be arranged in such a manner that, if the news editor wants to reduce length, he can clip from the end. In other words, the most important news should be arranged in the beginning and the less important in descending order. The shooting should be arranged through a professional producer on U-matic tapes. The TV stations accept only professional U-matic (3/4 inches) tapes and not half-inch unprofessional tapes or 16 mm and 35 mm spools. After the film footage is shot, the edited version will need a voicecast, music, etc., which should also be carefully selected. One can also send an edited clip with a written script indicating the visual input in the film alongside to enable the newsreader to lend his/her voice. On special occasions, say a landmark, a VIP visit, or a crisis situation like an accident, a fire, or sabotage, the TV team may approach the Public Relations person to allow shooting. Professionalism demands that after verifying the identities and authority letters of the TV station, the Public Relations practitioner should facilitate coverage by providing access to the place, information and management's viewpoint, should the coverage be after a crisis situation. As a proactive Public Relations, a Public Relations practitioner should plan in advance the occasions which demand sending news releases to TV stations.

2. *Mass Media:* The press, TV, radio, films, documentaries, outdoor (hoardings and posters) among others comprise the mass media. The mass media constitute a nation's public information system or mass communication, a system in which Public Relations plays an important role.

3. *Radio:* How can radio be used as a Public Relations medium? News bulletins are broadcast over the radio at fixed intervals throughout the day, both on national and local frequencies. Organisations can use the medium by sending press releases relating their performance and development. All India Radio's code, however, rules out the mention of the name of a private company in a news bulletin or newsreel. News is selected for broadcast based

on its news worthiness to the listeners. A radio news release should be written in radio style so that it can be used by an announcer without much editing.

4. *Film/Video:* The film, first the silent and then the talkie in the earlier part of this century, represents one of the most significant landmarks in the development of mass communication. The shift in our dependence from words to pictures has made all the difference to the way we think and perceive things.

Film/documentaries can be made on formats like 35 mm, 16 mm and video. As a Public Relations practitioner, one does not need to be an expert film-maker, but he should necessarily have a working knowledge of the medium. This will help him decide the line of approach, the format, the treatment and, of course, the budgeting and appropriation of funds, etc. Making films on celluloid in 35 mm or 16 mm format promises excellent results, but it is cumbersome, time-consuming and expensive. Unless the film is to be viewed by a very large audience in a theatre, video can easily replace celluloid. Video equipment has the advantage of playing back the image immediately. It does not need processing as in the case of film. It is also possible to reshoot on the same film if the results are not satisfactory. Synchronised sound is possible with every video recorder and if necessary different sound tracks can be superimposed on a sound track in different languages or dialects. Video tape can be redone by adding fresh coverage or by replacing some shots for updating the programme. Video has the choice of computer backed special effects.

In the last two-three decades, there have been many generations of video equipment—from low band to high band. Now it is beta chem, the latest state of art cameras and equipment. The cost of film also varies depending on the kind of equipment used. Video has its disadvantages also. The equipment is delicate and susceptible to moisture. Video tapes get jammed or damaged with repeated use. As compared to film, the video tape has a smaller life. As a Public Relations practitioner, one should have acquaintance with the equipment and studio to know about the options and capabilities of the medium. A couple of visits to a video studio is all that is required to gain a working knowledge of the medium.

5. *Outdoor Communication:* Outdoor communication has done to the environment and landscaping what no other medium has. It is impossible to ignore the loud messages staring at you from the large billboards, hoardings and posters as soon as you step out of your home. As the day graduates to dusk, some of the well known cities turn into a virtual kaleidoscope of colour, fantasy and imagery with neon signs blinking at you. Environmentalists all over have been crying themselves hoarse about the damage to the landscape, but outdoor medium is here to stay. Generally used as a secondary or complementary medium, outdoor has a great potential as a reminder medium. Its strength lies in being a mass medium with 24-hour exposure. Outdoor creates a bigger than life feeling with high penetration. It has, however, its drawbacks also. One has to restrict oneself to short, simple messages. High blowing winds cause damage to the boards, rain and storm can result in short circuiting of neon signs. Outdoor is not a selective medium but a non-intrusive one. It is not possible to gauge its impact per exposure opportunity on the audience. The biggest criticism, however, is that it obliterates the natural beauty of the environment. As a Public Relations medium, it rotates the audience to maximise audience delivery. It also promises graphic flexibility.

Compared to other mass media, outdoor works out cheaper. In fact, if we see in the Indian context, wall writing or painting on the wall, which costs next to nothing, and pasting of paper posters can serve as an excellent publicity medium.

The Government of India has a full-fledged outdoor publicity department which uses the medium for disseminating information about its policy, programmes and various social marketing issues.

6. The Press: Mostly regarded as as the Fourth Estate particularly in democratic, the press wields enormous power and clout in a society. In the life of an organisation, it plays a significant role, enabling it to reach out to various categories of external publics. The press, in fact, puts "third party endorsement" on the activities of an organisation. The source of news coverage and editorial content about different organisations in a newspaper can be both known and unknown. If used properly, the press can play a complementary role but if mishandled or when Public Relations is in the hands of immature practitioners, inept handling could lead to damaging the image of the organisation. Press relations are in fact the proverbial acid test for Public Relations practitioners. Many a Public Relations person has been fired for mishandling the press. To make Public Relations and the press complement each other is not impossible. The news is created by the doings of the organisation which in turn are articulated by the people authorised to do so. How faithful the news coverage is, depends on the power of articulation. The problem arises when organisations want news reported in a manner which is favourable to them and which will promote their objectives and will not cause them trouble, whereas the news media want news that will interest their readers.

Marlin Nobon, a Washington reporter, once remarked that a reporter has a "vested interest in chaos". Sensationalism, juicy copy, and newsworthy personalities rather than news occupy the minds of some journalists. A Public Relations practitioner, on the other hand, has a vested interest in projecting his organisation in a favourable light. Let us admit that a Public Relations practitioner is a paid advocate to influence the minds of the people. He cannot, however, get away giving false versions or concocting things. In this age of information, a Public Relations practitioner is just one source of information. A good scribe will not submit his copy based on just the official source.

In order to utilise a powerful medium like the press, it is very important for a Public Relations practitioner to know the press scene, the content of different publications, and the functioning of the press and establish working relations with the concerned reporters, news editors etc. The relationship between Public Relations and press is of mutual interdependence. With the changing market scenario and the growing importance of the capital market, coverage of the industry is a necessary component of newspapers. In order to be credible, it is important to be knowledgeable. The first step which the Public Relations person should take is to acquaint himself fully with the organisation he is working for. To begin with, he should develop his own organisation as his "beat". Secondly, the Public Relations person need not be a technical person, even if the organisation is technical in nature like companies producing scientific, chemical or precision products. His being a communication expert will help the organisation in putting across the most technical issues in the common man's language through the media. And the media appreciate contributions of this nature.

Press relations can't be built overnight. It is a continuous process. To be successful in this respect, a Public Relations person must go beyond the press release relationship. Press briefings and informal meets help develop a lasting relationship.

The Government of India has a large network of information officers in the Press Information Bureau. Headed by the Principal Information Officer, the information officers are attached to different ministries. Their Job is to provide information to the press regarding policies and performances of their ministries and the viewpoints of the legislature on different issues through their ministers. Public Relations practitioners working in the public sector and in government-funded organisations can utilise the services of the PIB to reach the nooks and corners of the country through their vast network.

Next comes Selective media are those media which are decided upon keeping in view the identifiable target audience. The audience can be employees, shareholders, wholesalers, consumers, opinion-makers and also some sections of the public at large. Let us discuss some of the media.

Channels for Employee Communication: This probably is the only branch of public relations in which the Public Relations practitioner has complete control. Internal communication often requires designing and producing the media material, which may include a whole range of employee magazines, films, AVs, instruction materials, safety manuals, corporate identity manuals, bulletin boards etc.

Marshal McLuhan, created quite a few ripples when he said that the form used for a communication is communication in itself. To illustrate, in times of a national crisis, if a TV station announces that the Head of the Government will address the nation on TV at such and such time, the audience would assume that some important or critical message is coming. In another case, if an employee receives a letter from the President of his company, even before opening the envelope he would expect some important communication. because through experience he knows that the President very rarely addresses the employees through mail. Many scholars, however, do not agree with McLuhan's theory. They argue that a medium may be a tip off about the quality and nature of the message but is not surely all the message. Access to a medium does not necessarily mean that the message has in reality reached the target audience. To illustrate, a newspaper is subscribed to by many but not all the news is read by all the people.

While creating channels of internal communication, a Public Relations practitioner has to weigh the pros and cons of all the media individually and collectively keeping in view the individual stimuli and group stimuli of the employees.

Let us have a look at some of the popular media for internal communication.

House Journal: A house journal or magazine as commonly referred to is a means of reaching a particular set of publics with certain written material at a particular periodicity.

There is no hard and fast rule as to what it should contain. In fact, the content depends on the overall environment of an organisation.

The house journal of an open company will have a two-way flow of communication between management and employees, while a look at the house journal of a closed company will reflect one-way communication. In other words, management communicating to employees.

A Public Relations practitioner should be careful to follow a conscious policy and formulate objectives when he plans to publish a house journal. He must bear in mind that communication is a means and not an end. A house journal, if carefully produced, serves as an important link between management and its various employees.

A house journal can cover topics in a number of areas and can be sent to employees as well as distributors, agents, opinion-makers and other external publics. Larger companies can have separate journals for internal and external publics. The bottom line for a house journal is to satisfy the needs and interests of its readers. A house journal in fact is about people, their interests, their hopes, their aspirations. It must satisfy their inquisitive minds. It should attempt to answer all by creating a healthy forum for expression of thought and vision of the management and employees. Human interest should be the governing principle for stories. Too many uninteresting figures and technical details are unlikely to interest readers.

Bulletin Boards: Conventionally, a bulletin board in an organisational context can be described as a stage for a continuous flow of news and messages concerning employees. They can be seen at shopfloors of organisations in various formats and sizes. Sometimes they are vertical, at other times horizontal or square. In some organisations they are drab-looking plain boards, while in others they are fancy, of cork surface with a good teak, walnut or stainless steel frame. Papers are stuck on to the board with pins; if it is metallic with little magnets. The messages stuck on the boards have more or less a fixed life. Professional Public Relations departments take pains in designing and preparing an interesting layout for their bulletin board. Before we discuss what it contains, let us analyse the objective of bulletin boards. Every office has a system of interacting with its employees on official matters. Circulars and memos are an essential part of the life of an average employee. Most of the circulars and memos that have relevance for a large number of employees are on issues concerning job, welfare activities, change in policies, etc.

These have also to be displayed on notice boards besides being circulated individually, if required. Apart from personnel news, bulletin boards have become a sought after medium by production heads/PR practitioners motivating employees to reach the production targets. Competition among different shifts is also encouraged by giving shiftwise production details on the bulletin boards. Bulletin boards at times also serve as an unofficial grapevine and centre for corporate intelligence/observation. While going in or coming out of the shopfloor, employees tend to gather around the bulletin boards to read the latest information. While being there, they also exchange views on a number of critical issues with their peer group and it is here that the group stimuli are at their peak.

The Closed-Circuit Television (CCTV): Closed-circuit or in-house TV is a good medium linking up a scattered audience. Cable TV has further cemented the bond of fellow feeling in corporate townships. The medium is cost effective, if there is personal involvement. Looking at the multi-dimensional impact of the audiovisual medium with a captive audience, it can work wonders, if ingenuity is used. Visuals within an organisation can be used to train, inform, motivate, and entertain. Some of the leading organisations — to name a few, National Thermal Power Corporation, Steel Authority of India and India Tobacco Company, have gone in for video magazines for employee communication. The contents include management's point of view on various issues, company performance, welfare measures, human interest stories, community Public Relations glimpses, etc. However, video magazines have not replaced printed house journals. They complement each other.

Annual Reports: Not long ago, annual reports were drab-looking journals without much thought given about their presentation. Not any more. Annual reports have come to be recognised as an important Public Relations tool for corporate communication. With more and more organisations going public, you need more annual reports to send to the shareholders. Although the Public Relations department of a company does not have a direct responsibility for preparing the balance-sheet and the statements of accounts, it does advise the management on the overall approach of the report, the theme of the chairman's statement and on the format and presentation of the report.

One must invite a professional advertising/ designing agency to handle the assignment. The profile of the company during the year under review can be befittingly projected in the director's report which can have diagrams, pie charts, and pictures of developmental activities of your company. Care should be taken to choose a printer who has the expertise in printing annual reports. As bringing out annual reports is a statutory requirement and it should be published before the annual general meeting, a strict time schedule must be worked out with the printer.

In fact most of the printers are busy printing annual reports of different companies at the same time, hence one must select a printer who has the capacity to undertake and deliver the job on time. One should plan to the minutest detail. As the annual report contains the balance-sheet, be careful about proof-reading. It is advisable to get the final proofs cleared from the Company Secretariat Department which has prepared the manuscript and the statement of accounts.

Printed Literature

It is rare that an organisation, whether in the product or the service line, does not need publicity literature to promote its products and activities. In fact, printed literature can be segmented into various ways such as the brochures, leaflets, booklets, direct mail etc. All have the same objective, i.e., to inform or persuade the audience about an idea or a service.

1. Brochure: A brochure is a multipanel publication that conveys information usually on a single subject. A brochure is also called a pamphlet, a dyer or a folder. A booklet serves much the same purpose as a brochure except that it has more pages that may be stapled together rather than folded. Organisations need brochures and booklets for a variety of reasons — to explain a new programme, a process, a product, a new building or plant, or a laboratory, to ask for donations, or to sell a product by describing its virtues. Such publications are reasonably inexpensive, relatively fast to produce, and are attractive to read, if prepared carefully. Although as a Public Relations practitioner you will have the services of a professional designer or a professional agency to go about the job, it is important to know the basics in order to be able to guide the production.

A brochure has an overall size with fold configuration like four panel, six panel, eight panel and so on. In deciding on the number of folds, remember that ease of reader comprehension is important. Brochures need to be folded in such a manner that they can be easily opened and copy read from one panel to another. Copy or the text is the most important part of the brochure. It is not possible to write long copy because of the size of the brochure. Identify the person who will write the copy. He can be from within the organisation or from an advertising agency. The copywriter must be given the right brief so that he can develop the text. Pictures, graphs, charts must also be selected carefully to go with the copy.

Other Publicity and Promotional Literature

In the face of tough competition in the market place, where similar products vie with each other, it is necessary to promote the products or services continuously. Consumer durables and capital goods need large amount of support literature in contrast with small items like chocolates, candy bars or ice-creams. With modern retailing techniques, products have to really sell themselves. This has led to aggressive publicity at the point of purchase or retail outlets.

Direct Mail

Direct mail in some circumstances is the most powerful and certainly the most cost effective. It uses the postal service to deliver messages to a selected target audience. In fact, it is also called selective marketing technique. The receiver of the direct mail literature is generally invited to send for further information and/or to ask for some kind of personal call to provide a demonstration or to give further details of the product being offered. Hotel chains, investment agents, etc., use it as a means of keeping in communication with their regular clients. Direct mail is both a selective and a flexible medium which makes it cost effective. It is selective because it is addressed to those and only those people whom you want to reach. It is flexible because the number of letters you mail can be increased or reduced according to the capacity of your sales force to cope with enquiries. Direct mail can be a friendly and personal medium of reaching out to a specific target audience. Direct mail has its limitations also. If you want it to be effective, make the list of the target audience carefully. Building a good list usually entails a great deal of research and keeping it up to date, calls for concerted effort.

MEDIA RELATIONS

Media relations form the most basic activity of public relations. Media relations, in fact, take a good part of the practitioner's working day and are exacting in their demands.

Some of the tools for maintaining effective media relations are organising press conferences, holding press briefings and arranging press visits or facility tours for the media men. Let us discuss these one by one.

Press Conference

As a Public Relations practitioner, you will be solely responsible for organising press conferences. A press conference is generally used as an occasion for the release of news simultaneously to all media, provided the subject is newsworthy.

When should you organise a press conference? The answer is — not very frequently. Do not fall for the temptation of calling a press conference, if the subject does not demand a discussion between your organisation's spokesperson and the media. In such a case, a press release will do the job. If however, your organisation has to announce a major policy, speak about a labour-management rift, or launch a product which requires demonstration — things that would suggest the need for a face to face dialogue and not a one-side statement — then call a press conference.

Guidelines

- A decision about the spokesperson who will address the press conference. Remember, the Public Relations person himself should never address a press conference. It should ideally be the head of the organisation or of a department
- Prepare a press kit which must contain a press backgrounder, a news release or releases, pictures, literature about the organisation, a writing pad and a pen or pencil
- Make the list of invitees from the media carefully. The list should comprise those who cover your organisation.
- Decide a venue which is suitable for the media persons to reach.
- Make arrangements for the transport of media persons from a convenient place to the venue and for the return journey.
- Decide on the timing. It should neither be too early nor too late in the day. The conference should end at such a time that the media persons are able to get back to their place of work to file the story on time.
- Arrange hospitality.

In fact, as a Public Relations person, you should control the press conference from start to finish. After the chief spokesperson and the media persons have taken their seats, give your self-introduction and introduce the spokesperson who will be addressing. After a brief address by the spokesperson on the subject matter, it is thrown open to the media persons to ask questions. Set a time frame for the press conference to continue. Depending on the occasion, the ideal duration should be between 45 minutes and one hour. When the time is nearing completion, you can announce that there is time for, say, two questions or so. Normally, after setting the conference in motion, take a seat and do not intervene, but at times you may have to interject to rescue the spokesperson who may have been pushed into a corner by a reporter's question. Establish a personal rapport with the media persons. This cannot be achieved in a day but requires concerted efforts over a period of time. Press conference should not be the only occasion you meet them. It serves your cause better if you have a friendly press.

Press Briefings

Press briefings are different from press conferences in that they are informal and do not require elaborate arrangements. Press briefings can be both proactive and reactive. By proactive, it is meant that certain clarifications or points are required to be given after a crisis situation. In this case, some media persons are invited for press briefings.

In the case of critical issues, besides an informal briefing given by the spokesperson, a written statement is also handed over to avoid misquotation. In case of reactive press briefings, a pressman seeks an audience with the chief spokesperson for seeking certain clarifications or to have his point of view before filing the story. Similarly the spokesperson may have been misquoted, and he invites press men for clarifications.

Exhibitions

Exhibitions cover a very diverse series of events, ranging from major international trade fairs to small local activities organised by a community. An exhibition can be general in nature or specific. You must be aware of the India International Trade Fair which is organised every year by the Trade Fair Authority of India at Pragati Maidan in New Delhi. The fair begins on November 14 every year for a period of two weeks. Among the participants are Indian states, some foreign countries, and public and private sector companies. On display are products and activities through the multi-media approach. Trade between countries and different companies is also conducted. The TFAI also organises exhibitions and fairs on specific themes from time to time, like engineering goods fair, electronics exhibition, sports goods fair, textile fair, to name a few. Exhibitions can be a very powerful medium of communication, if handled properly. The medium helps publicise the image of the country. It can become a meeting place for existing customers and potential customers and can identify new sales areas/outlets. New products can be introduced and the feedback of the customer can be had instantly. It also helps assess the performance of the competitors in terms of product, service and presentation.

Press Tours

In press tours or facility visits, much of the exercise is similar to organising a press conference. More elaborate arrangements are however required to be made as it may involve transporting the press party a long distance. The occasion could be a landmark achieved, the commissioning of a project or a crisis situation like an accident. Both occasions need careful planning and organisation. While inviting a reporter to join your press tour, it is always advisable to write to the editors or chiefs of the bureau of different newspapers. In normal circumstances, sufficient notice must be given, because the concerned reporter may have to be spared for a number of days from the place of work.

Open Days

"Open day" is an important tool to build rapport with the community/ neighbourhood where the plant is located. It is also a traditional way of building pride and morale among your employees and their families. The Public Relations department organises visits of employees' families and of the community at large to the plant to see the product manufacturing and other facets of a plant on a few days in a year which are referred as "open days". Such visits are accompanied by hospitality by the plant owners. It is important, however, to make suitable arrangements to receive visitors. This entails not only the provision of trained guides but also hospitality, etc. It is usual in many industry conducted tours to provide refreshments to visitors at the end of the tour. If however, the factory is situated out of town, and it has taken long for the visitors to reach there, it is advisable to offer refreshments on arrival. Factories producing eatables generally not only offer the visitors their items in refreshments but may also present gift packs.

Special Events

In planning special events, large or small, it is important to have a management structure that is ultimately responsible for the event, and make timely decisions. The event itself needs publicity for better response from the target audience.

It can be said that there are various media available to a Public Relations practitioner to reach the various publics, his organisation has to deal with from time to time. Broadly, the publics of a company comprise the employees, the shareholders, the dealers, the stockists, the customers, the government, the media and the public at large.

In fact the message, the media and the audience have to be matched to get the desired impact. For reaching out to the public at large, we need to use the mass media like the TV, radio and films. Through the medium of house journals, we can reach both internal and external publics. In order to promote the products or the services of a company, various types of promotional literature like brochure, point of purchase material and direct mail can be made use of.

Through exhibitions, trade fairs, special events and open houses, we can attract people to appreciate our activities. The products can be demonstrated, and the activities can be shown through working models to attract attention.

Media relations form on important part of Public Relations activities. In fact, it is through the media that we can reach out to a large audience without spending much.

Today the media scene in India is paradoxical. The number of journals and newspapers is going up, the quality of production is also going up, and the awareness of and hunger for news are increasing. Yet circulation is going down. Obviously other factors are at work, like inflation, the question of credibility, cynicism about and disillusionment with the political, social or economic system, etc.

The number of journals and newspapers on December 31, 1991, was 30,214 compared to 28,491 on December 31, 1990, an increase of 3.7 per cent. Among them, 3,229 were dailies, 257 tri-or bi-weeklies, 9,621 weeklies and 17,107 other periodicals. Newspapers were brought out in 93 languages and dialects (*Registrar of Newspapers of India*).

Quality wise, magazines like *India Today* can compare with any periodical anywhere in the world. Dailies like the *Telegraph,* the *Pioneer* and the *Independent* can also compare in content, layout and design and presentation with dailies anywhere.

In the electronic media the number of radio stations swelled to 144, covering nearly 85 per cent of the country's area and 95.7 per cent of the population. However the number of radio/transistor sets per 100 persons was only 4.4. The total number of radio/transistor sets was 3 crore but 80 per cent of them were in urban homes. There were only 60 lakh sets for the 52.5 crore population in backward or inaccessible rural areas. Though television has expanded dramatically since the 1982 Asiad, most of the 1.1 crore sets are in urban areas, with the bigger cities claiming the lion's share. Which means TV is truly a class medium in a country in which the mass media are mostly accessible only to the relatively more affluent.

Notably, Cinema has limited reach, influencing largely the urban population or the rural elite. India produces 900 feature films annually. But there are only 11,200 cinema houses with 11.5 lakh seats—3.4 seats per 1000 of population. Cable TV likewise services largely or only the elite. By the first quarter of 1991 there were about 10,000 cable TV operators, almost all of them confined to urban areas, according to a survey carried out by the Indian Institute of Mass Communication.

In the print medium, growing news awareness, improved packaging and the demand of consumers for better quality, a rat race has developed among newspapers for a greater slice of the stagnant or diminishing cake. The struggle is on simultaneously in many areas. Newspapers are becoming more voluminous, carrying more news from more areas about more things. Since those who read newspapers, specially in the larger towns and cities (which account for 93 per cent of the readership of dailies), are increasingly being rushed for time, this means that most news items are being read by the headline alone and many by the headline plus intro (first paragraph or first two paragraphs).

This has led newspapers to give increasingly expressive headlines. Unfortunately, this sometimes tends to degenerate into sensationalism. Intros are also packing in more facts, and again the temptation to put in the more sensational aspect of the news sometimes gets the better of the subeditor's judgment.

One purpose of skeletonising news items is to induce readers to "enter" the item undeterred by its length. The other is to make room for specialist reports/columns/ articles which readers seem to hunger for. A third purpose is to make room for "Entry Points" — blurbs, visuals, cartoons, sketches, graphs, pictures etc.

A major by-product of the rat race among newspaper is what is called "investigative" reporting. Some eminent journalists like S. Nihal Singh — he was a five-star reporter in his time — say this is a misnomer because all reporting has to be investigative. However, it is a fact that reporters, driven by their Editors to bring in "scoops", are nowadays doing more and deeper investigation than before into news points that they come across through handouts, by word of mouth or in any other way.

This, and the realisation of the enormous power of the media, has led to "sources" in government and private organisations leaking sensitive information to reporters. Sometimes these "sources" are driven only by the desire to take part in the exciting media game or to correct a distortion. But very often the motive is ulterior — to gain personal advantage or to *"fix"* someone. There is no objection to obtaining leaks from lower-level officials in Government and business organisations. But to treat them as the gospel or to use them without cross-checking and without finding out the context is unprofessional.

Such unprofessionalism is becoming increasingly common feature. The reason is that reporters are increasingly under pressure to obtain "scoops", either from their Editors in order to be one up on other papers, or from their keenness to be known as "scoopsters". It so happens that reporters with a larger number of "scoops" and bylines move ahead much faster than those who are quiet and painstaking gatherers of unspectacular news, even though the unspectacular news is the staple diet of newspapers. From the point of view of the Public Relations professional this is a disturbing scenario. For, it is difficult enough for the Public Relations person to give a scoop every day, or even every week or every month, to the media. More complications arise because of the "scoopster" syndrome.

The first complication is that, hell-bent on getting a scoop, many reporters (even newspapers) are falling for the temptation of presenting one side of the picture to gain circulation/populist mileage. A large number of newspapers and magazines are acquiring what is called a "policy" for news — to select news which favours or disfavours a particular cause, party, industry, even business group! This is in contrast with the earlier dictum: "News is sacred, comment is free". This development — along with other changes in the information milieu — has not failed to influence readers. In contrast with, say, three or even two decades ago, readers have progressively been becoming ready to change over to the more juicy newspaper.

With the phenomenal growth of trade and industry, advertising revenue has swelled, making for new found prosperity for the more competent and/or more juicy of the daily newspapers. Faster communication (more teleprinter lines, computerised creeding, etc., air-freighting of copies of newspapers) has meant wider scope for circulation and advertising.

The recent magazine boom, including the Sunday newspaper movement, based on (i) in-depth reportage; (ii) research; (iii) colour; and (iv) speedier distribution has added another dimension to the change. Magazines and Sunday papers cannot compete with dailies in the matter of spot news.

Thus the Public Relations person's responsibility and importance increases manifold in this new media environment. Earlier the Public Relations person was one whose job was just to keep in touch with the media. Now his job is to be first with his version to the media, to pre-empt distortions and to correct them when they occur. The are lights of the media are now constantly focused on everyone. It is the job of the Public Relations person to ensure that they pick up the right images without distortions.

Public Relations Opportunities

Consider the external publics — the consumer of your product, the people living in the neighbourhood of your chemicals factory with all the attendant risks, the Government functionaries who oversee the functioning of such factories, those who supply the raw materials etc. A four-inch news item in newspapers about the factory can influence their behaviour as much as thousands of words of sales talk, or advertising, or meetings, or telephonic conversation. This is so even if the news item cites only anonymous sources whereas the sales talk is delivered or the meeting is chaired by the head of your organisation.

Even internal publics — like workers of your factory, or your sales agents — will react to the four-inch news item. If the item talks of the danger of a gas leak, the people in the neighbourhood and your own workers may hold a demonstration or send in petitions. If on the other hand, the item talks of a 25 per cent rise in sales, morale will rise sky-high. It follows, therefore, that everyone practising public relations, which includes both wholetime Public Relations persons and those in production, R and D and sales, should study the media scene closely.

The Public Relations person must, therefore, know when it is the right time for his organisation's news to land at the Chief Sub's desk. Which means he must feed the information to the reporter sufficiently in advance to enable him to prepare his report on time. There is, then, contingency planning to be done. The reporter may be given the information just in time, but he may have one other important report to write and a third news item to chase before the world goes to bed.

It is possible to feed the information long before time to the reporter on the understanding that though the report may be ready it will be released to the desk just at the right time — not too early and not too late. This is called the embargo. This is specially useful when the Public Relations person and the reporter concerned have a good rapport with each other.

The premise to start from is that both the Public Relations person and the reporter need each other. Without the reporter the Public Relations person is without the medium through which to operate. Without the Public Relations person, the reporter is without his source. Okay, he can obtain rumours, leaks, bits of information from malcontents in the organisation, from staff who have only heard of the facts, parts of facts, etc. But there is, or can be, no substitute for an authentic, credible and reliable news source. No matter what non-newsmen think, all reporters all over the world value trustworthy news sources above mere informants, rumour-mongers and malcontents. This puts the ball squarely in the court of the Public Relations person. The reporter needs him, yes, but the Public Relations person needs the reporter more. One day's newspaper carries 300 to 500 news items. It wants your organisation's news item for today's edition, but if the worst comes to the worst the edition will be locked up without it — with regret. For the Public Relations person, that news item is the day's crucial output. Maybe there is another one, but that's about all.

Infact, Public Relations is basically a continuing and proactive process. Though Keats was a great poet and a famous thinker, no Public Relations person can follow his famous lines and go to sleep. Theperson's work is like nursing a constituency — unobtrusively, carefully, continuously. This way one can head off a crisis, or if a crisis develops the Public Relations person finds his constituents — meaning the media persons he has been nursing — standing up for him. If the Public Relations person neglects to nurse his constituents, he may find himself standing forlorn and unaided in a crisis. And yet, too much of a good thing can be dangerous. You should know how a newspaper works, about its deadlines etc. But it is rank bad Public Relations to tell a reporter "Take it, your deadline is at hand", or "Why do you need this information? It isn't necessary for the story". A disgusted business reporter once commented: "A lot of them (PR persons) think they have a right to lecture you about what a good story is!" [Quoted by Grabowski, "The Seven Deadly Sins of Media Relaitons"].

Another psychologically disastrous step a Public Relations person can take is to try to spoonfeed a reporter. Give all the information he needs and all that you think he can use. But do not dictate the story. Let the reporter think he is the one doing it.

Expectations of the Media

1. Reporters expect nothing to be hidden from them. If an attempt is made to hide something, it becomes counter-productive. This is because reporters are now so alert and have so many diverse sources that one or the other reporter is bound to find out. If there is something confidential, it is up to the executive to say, "Sorry, I cannot disclose it because our competitors would come to know." Give the correct reason.

2. The media expect up to date information from the Public Relations and other executives of public sector and other organisations. If the information is not up to date, reporters are bound to tap other sources. If these other sources give garbled or inaccurate information, it is the Public Relations person who is to blame. The reporter has a job to accomplish within a deadline. If the Public Relations person fails him, be will tap other sources.

3. If the information is late, reporters are bound to tap other sources—like members of the organisation not authorised to speak for it, malcontents in the organisation and those who have a personal or other axe to grind. This tends to reduce the executive to a defensive position where he tries to deny or correct half-truths, rumours and/or motivated or one-sided information. This is most damaging to the organisation. Dr Goebbels, Hitler's Propaganda

Minister, worked on this theory with considerable success. He would invent stories of German successes or Allied setbacks in the fighting and get them broadcast repeatedly. People who heard these stories again and again tended to believe that at least some of it was true. This was despite blanket Allied denials. What Goebbels did not realise is what Abraham Lincoln discovered more than a century earlier: "You cannot fool all the people all the time". The golden rule is that the news must come, first from the executive and should be as complete as possible. This will make reporters discount rumours/half-truths.

4. A fact little known in public sector organisations is that there are a series of deadlines in a newspaper. If the news you are giving is worth an inside page or local page, it should be given two to three hours earlier than news which can go on Page 1. The executive is therefore expected to give such news earlier than news which will in any case make Page 1.

5. With the increased role of graphics, it has become imperative for the executives or Public Relations person of public sector or other such organisations to be prepared with pictures/graphics/pie diagrams etc.

6. Make up your mind whether what you want to give is spot news, background, or information for a feature. In every case, but more particularly for a feature, collect and keep ready comparative facts and figures from the past or from other countries. The media expect such material.

7. Newspapers are perpetually struggling to fit in as much of news as possible into a limited amount of space. Remember that they have to carry (i) international news, (ii) national news, (iii) local news, (iv) business news, (v) regional news, (vi) sports news, (vii) cartoons, comments,

features. Therefore, it is not admissible to load them with all kinds of details in which their readers will not be interested. The executive must give the salient features of what his company is doing at the moment and in which the readers of the particular publication will be interested, leaving out the unnecessary details unless asked for. Remember that space costs money in newspapers and magazines and time costs money on TV/radio.

5

MIS & Public Relations in Public Administration

In fact, the concept of public relations as a component of public administration is as old as the world itself. Mughal Emperor Jehangir had bells of justice for aggrieved citizens to ring for an audience with the king. All that is new in public relations is proliferation of the idea consequent upon growth of organisations, industrialisation and diversification of modern business, on the one hand, and the availability of new means of communication, on the other. The former created the need for PR, the new mass media provided the tools. In the 19th century, there was expansion of industry and commerce in Europe and America, and the concomitant evils of urbanisation followed. There was conflict between agriculture and industry, between industry and government, and between government and the people. And to bring about harmony, it became necessary to have a tuning agency. And this came in through what has come to be known as public relations.

Public relations, a phenomenon of growth, seeks to resolve group-conflicts. The *International Encyclopedia of Social Sciences* defines public relations as "the organised effort to communicate information, and to modify attitudes or behaviour on behalf of a client, or a cause." Public relations is a sustained effort for mutual understanding. It is a philosophy of management—an attitude of mind—that aims at achieving a better understanding between an organisation and its public: employees, shareholders, customers, suppliers, dealers, etc.

It must be noted that public relations is not propaganda. Propaganda is a conscious effort to influence the opinions and actions of others. It may prove good when used for a worthy causes. It may be bad when used in stirring up hatred. Propaganda is only outward directed, but public relations is a two-way approach.

Also it must be noted again that 'Public Relations' is not mere publicity. Nor is it all puffery. At one time, public relations ended with publicity, but now public relations programmes embrace all those factors which impinge on one another in the relations of an organisation with its public—both internal and external. In government, public relations helps formation of sound public policies, and keeps employees morale high.

Process of Public Relations

Primarily, the public relations process consists of four steps: (i) fact-finding, (ii) planning, (iii) communication, and (iv) evaluation.

Fact-finding determines the public towards whom public relations programmes are to be beamed, so that public relations effort is not misdirected. Research determines the best way of reaching the public. And both these require adequate communication channels for two-way flow of information.

(i) Facts can be gathered from public offices, from libraries, from trade journals and newspapers. Then, there are informal sources like telephone and incoming mail. Advisory committees comprising public representatives also provide informative feedback.

(ii) Planning involves long-range programmes to achieve public relations mission and, within that wider framework, short-term plans operate to achieve, specific projects. Once a programme has been drawn, it is essential to associate top echelons of management with the plan so that they do not remain uninformed. In fact, a careful briefing at all levels is important.

(iii) Communication, the third step is most vital. Communication has three basic elements: the sender of the message, the message itself, and the receiver of the message. The fact that 'people" are a common factor in all public relations activities is an important consideration in tailoring communication programmes. Communication disseminates knowledge is the chief requisite to change in our society, and it also has the much needed leavening effect. Communication is, therefore, one of the primary factors in the process of development.

This involves empathic listening. We learn far more by listening than by talking, for we can only talk about things we already know. Listening is largely a mental process. A Confucian saying has it that God has given two ears and one mouth so that man may listen more, and speak less.

(iv) Evaluation is the final step in the public relations process. An extensive review is essential to judge the effectiveness of a programme. Evaluation of a public relations programme is a complex exercise, and measurement of gains does not readily offer an arithmetical answer. The benefits accrue more in terms of changed attitudes.

Funding Public Relations

Of prime importance is the fact that, 'Public Relations' activities cost a lot of money. But this is investment—like money spent on acquiring good plant and machinery. And as effective public relations involves sustained long-term endeavour, an insufficient allocation of funds of public relations would be extravagance.

Public Relations in Government

It must be noted that in modern times democracy cannot function in isolation and insulation from its public. And a well-informed and responsive citizenry is fundamental to the achievement of government's goals. Public has been defined as "any loose association of individuals who are held together by common interest and objectives, and by various means of communication." In a vast country, the government's public would be large and heterogeneous. And its structure would be complex and varied. There would be the urban public and the rural public; men, women, and youth public; land-owners and landless farmers. Public would be groupable by religion, by occupation, and by language. There would also be classification by business, profession, and by educational patterns.

And no less important is the internal public—the multitude of employees over whom the government extends its benign umbrella. They are government's greatest asset, and its best ambassadors.

It would be an exaggeration to speak of 'relation' between government and its public. For, there are various types of administration. Some perform services for the citizen, like railways and post offices; whereas others impose levies, like tax offices and octroi posts. Still others enforce the rule of law and impose constraints, like the police administration. Many an element goes into the making of public administration e.g., policy and planning, budget and finance, purchase and sale, supervision and control and public relations *et al.* All these are inter-related; none is independent. And a good administration blends and harmonises these elements.

Remarkably, Public Relations status of government as a whole would be only as high as the amount of public respect enjoyed by its weakest agency. Hence, the need for every department to project a uniformly high image of the government.

Evidently, Public relations is no substitute for performance, and a public relations programme will not succeed if public services are deficient. Good public relations begins where the citizen 'meets' the administration. A public official must be socially sensitive to people's needs and aspirations. He must show consideration for the citizen's time, and meet him on an equal footing while transacting public business. Courtesy in written communications is important, and so is the promptness of replies. Similarly, forms and procedures, like a good sermon, must be easily understandable by the humblest of men. Then, the cooperative effort of the citizens would form an important link in the country's development.

During the British rule in India, the dignity of the human being was neglected within the government apparatus as well as outside. Those false old values: the gnawing superiority of the boss, his condescending attitude, the indifference to public needs, the narrow window-openings at public counters that disembody the clients, and those brass bars—all generate outlook passive attitudes among employees, and the citizens.

Webster's *Third New International Dictionary* defines bureaucracy *inter alia* as "...a system of administration marked by constant striving for increased functions and power, by lack of initiative and flexibility, by indifference to human needs or public opinion, and by a tendency to defer decisions to superiors or to impede action with red tape...." The objective of public relations endeavour should, therefore, be to humanise administration, and to make it sensitive to public opinion. The employees also need to be sold, not merely told.

In India, Public administration is not a new invention. It has been in existence for hundreds of years. But it has acquired three new features after Independence:

(a) Its purpose has been completely re-oriented—there is a shift from rule to service.
(b) Its function has been enormously increased—in number, in variety, and in complexity.
(c) Its methodology is changing—from trial-and-error method to modern management techniques.

In government, public relations programmes should be designed for achieving one or more of the following objectives:

(i) arousing citizens' interest in their government, and helping them better understand the rationale behind public policies;
(ii) bringing about change in the attitude of public officials for better employer-employee relations, and for ensuring citizen-oriented public services;
(iii) winning social acceptance for new legislation;
(iv) keeping citizens informed of the services available for them;
(v) motivating active participation of citizens in implementation of new economic and welfare programmes;
(vi) improving inter-state and international relations;

(vii) organising preventive/preparatory public relations before launching new measures of public importance; and

(viii) improving voluntary compliance of tax law;

(ix) eradicating social evils, like casteism and dowry;

(x) selling a new department of government, thus ensuring its staying in business (e.g., Department of Tourism);

(xi) providing means of feedback for top government authorities;

The most remarkable contribution of public relations lies in the fact that it bridges the communication gap, and establishes harmony between an organisation and its public. Public relations is continuous process. The results of its endeavours may not surface immediately, but progressively, and over a period of time.

In the context of present time, there is an urgent need of effective and affirmative public relations in public administration. Management information system plays crucial role in this. Coordination among these is cry of hour.

Good public relations will sell the service, and improve its tone.

REFERENCES

Gadgil, D.R. (1965), *Planning and Economic Policy in India*, Poona, Gokhale Institute of Politics and Economics.

King, J.A. (Jr.) (1967), *Economic Development Projects and Their Appraisal,* Baltimore, Johns Hopkins Press.

Little, I.M.D. and Mirrlees, J.A. (1969), *Manual of Industrial Projects Analysis in Developing Countries.* Vol. II, Paris, Organisation for Economic Cooperation and Development.

6

Role of Writing in Public Relations

The Public Relations personnel, while writing for the media, is simultaneously advocating his organisation's cause without letting it show. The prime motive of writing is not only to inform but simultaneously to persuade and motivate the audience. However, if it degenerates into blatant propaganda, the public relations person and his organisation both lose credibility.

FORMS OF WRITING

A. Press Releases

As the core of spirit, writing a press release consists of balancing two seemingly conflicting considerations — projecting the organisation's achievements and giving the news points which will appeal to the readers of the newspaper. For, while his organisation is all important for the public relations man, the acid test for the newspaper reporter or News Editor is what will be informative for his readers.

The seeming conflict between the two objectives is, however, no conflict at all in most cases. The reasons are two. *First,* one writes a press release when one has something new to say, and this is what the reporter or News Editor is looking for. *Second,* the purpose of writing a press release is not to show the boss the range or quality of one's writing but to get the news published. Far too many public relations persons write to impress the boss, and this is reflected not only in the news points they choose to project but in the presentation.

Another crucial point to be noted for all those writing press releases is that the very first sentence is so worded as to put off any reporter or News Editor, harried as he is by a deadline. All public relations persons must know that the Newsroom of a newspaper is bombarded with so much wordage that the key man (the News Editor or the Chief Sub) is just able to taste copy. That is, he looks at the dateline, the first sentence or paragraph, and throws a glance down the page to see if anything important catches the eye.

Of course, one can argue that any News Editor who rejects a news item after reading the first few words is being shallow, lazy or worse. But let us remember that it takes all kinds to make this world. There can be lazy, methodical, disorganised, meticulous and other kinds of News Editors. The public relations man must deal with the News Editors he finds. His job is not to reform the world (or to reform all News Editors) but to put across the company's point of view in such a way that it is published and reaches the reader. The target audience is the reader, the newspaper is the channel and the News Editor only the intermediary who can help you get into this channel.

This brings us to the structuring of a press release. Given the fact of copy tasting, the press release must pack the company's USP — namely that it has broken new ground by raising profit faster than sales — in the very first para, which journalists call the "intro". The "intro" consists of that news point which is the reason for writing the press release and on which one would like the headline to be based. It would, inevitably, be the most important news point in the press release. This is called the projection.

Having decided on what the "Intro" would contain, one should go step by step as follows:

1. Writing a press release essentially consists of selecting the more important news points for use while rejecting the less important points.
2. The point with the highest news value comes first.

Whichever of the points of a press note or news story you would like the headline to be based on, that comes in the "intro". Other points follow in logical sequence.

3. *Presentation:* The next step should follow from the first; the third from the second; and so on.
4. The length should be manageable and short. Generally, if your press release threatens to overflow from Page 1 to the turn page, it is untidy. Try to confine it to a length which can be carried conveniently on one page without occupying a disproportionate amount of space.
5. Notably, in newspapers, space is one constraint and time is another. In every newspaper the News Editor or Chief Subeditor tries to confine the length of an item to fit a particular space. If at the last moment the item is longer, the Chief Sub would rather cut a sentence/ paragraph from the bottom than miss the deadline.

Here it must be kept in mind that write in such a way that the last sentence/last para/last two paragraphs can be dropped without doing violence to the story. As per practice, never put an important/vital point in the last two paragraphs.

Points to Remember

A. Your handout/press release will be competing with News Agency copy/Staff Reporter copy/ Special Correspondent copy for space. Therefore, keep it short, crisp, to the point and written in such a way as to give the reader the sensation of change.

B. Your handout/press release will also be competing for time with other news items. If both handout and Staffer Copy are late, the Chief Sub will tend to prefer Staffer copy.

[Make sure your handout reaches the News Editor/ Chief Sub well before the deadline for the particular edition/ page. Make an estimate of which edition or page your item is likely to make.]

C. Space costs money in newspapers and time costs money on TV/radio. The more compact your copy, the greater its chances of publication.

D. The less of effort by way of editing/rewriting your press release needs, the greater the chances of use.

Types of Press Release

1. *Announcement release:* A new product, the opening of a new plant, the latest financial results, a new company policy, etc, can be occasions for issuing an announcement release. While deciding to write a news release of this kind, ask yourself what is so unique about your product or policy which will interest the reader of the newspaper. Ask yourself honestly if an advertisement is required to make the announcement or it needs "third party endorsement". Sometimes both are needed. Just manufacturing a "me-too" product is not enough reason

for issuing an announcement release. If your product has a Unique Selling Proposition (USP) or something which no similar product has, then there can be a case for a press release.

2. *Spot news release:* Significantly, while an announcement and a created news release can be planned in advance, a spot news release often does not give much time to the public relations man. Such releases are in response generally to a crisis situation like an accident, a hijack, a sabotage, an unrest etc. In such cases the public relations person has to work like a newspaper reporter, meeting deadlines and gathering the information quickly before unauthorised people speak to the newspapers.

3. *"Created News" release:* An announcement often is not attractive enough to catch media attention. As stated, right at the start of this chapter, the public relations man's writing differs from the reporter's in that it advocates the cause of his organisation. Consequently some amount of "dressing" up to get good coverage is legitimate. For instance, a public relations person may invite well known personalities to a company function or for the formal release of a product. This gives the public relations person something interesting to say — and the reporter to anchor his story.

4. *Response release:* The media have many sources of news and often news about an organisation reaches the media from sources other than the public relations department. A consumer group may issue a critical report about the organisation. Some investigating agencies may issue a damaging report. A research group may ublish a major study on your organisation's working, or a comment about the organisation may be made by a public figure. A competitor in an interview to the media can take a swipe

at your organisation. There can be occasions for issuing a response release. Organisations with professional public relations persons anticipate such events and as a proactive measure keep the response ready. The response release may be a brief statement, or a full-fledged news release giving the organisation's position in detail. Even if a response is not sought, keeping silent may mean accepting what is written. It is advisable to issue a release giving the organisation's point of view immediately.

5. *Bad news release:* Sometimes events occur that a company would like to keep silent about and not open the pandora's box by volunteering to give news. Most organisations feel if they keep silent nobody would know. On the other hand if they speak they would unnecessarily get a minus point noted. Yet, silence may backfire. For the media frequently get a story from sources other than public relations. If such is the scenario, the organisation would be admired for informing the people on its own about the accident or loss of life or whatever.

6. *Feature release:* A newspaper is more than a record of events that happened yesterday. Development stories and features on topical issues occupy much space in today's newspapers. Public relations practitioners can work at leisure on this aspect by finding feature material somewhere in their organisation, say in research and development, conservation measures, etc. Feature releases are generally "exclusives", which should not be distributed to all but to that newspaper or magazine which wants to use them. For this the public relations person has to make preliminary soundings.

B. Press Notes

The relationship between the reporter and the public relations person is symbiotic. That is, not everything is said formally or in writing. Often a reporter, not very satisfied with tid bits dropped into his lap by the chief executive or the public relations person, may remark off the cuff to the public relations person that he would want a complete picture. Or he may ask which exact methods of inventory control were used. If he is smart, he would prepare detailed press notes full of facts which the reporter wants. Such a press note need not be circulated to all reporters, for it is deemed to have been prepared on request. If, however, a rival reporter complains, the public relations person should be ready to offer to prepare for him a press note full of facts on another aspect of the company's operations on an exclusive basis. It is true that the public relations person is required to treat all reporters equally. But this equality is like the equality among different students in a class. The teacher may have to spend more time and energy on one student than on another. It is false equality to say that he would do exactly as much for one student as for another—just as the mother cannot say she would give equal food to all her children regardless of their individual needs.

There are things like annual financial results in which all papers will be interested. They should be prepared as a press release and distributed to everyone, though some will use a quarter of it, some half, some all of it and some may want to add more facts by making further inquiries. The reason is that not all newspapers or magazines have an identical audience — even those papers or magazines which seem to be competing with each other.

The advantage that the public relations man gets is that he is depended upon by reporters to give them not only general news items distributed to everyone but exclusives. In the chapter on the media scene, we have seen how an increasing number of reporters today live and advance in their trade through exclusives or "scoops". It is said that a good reporter has always an exclusive up his sleeve which he should be able to deliver within hours of being told that the Communication Package of a particular edition or section is not exciting enough. What this means is that the reporter has contacts who can give him an exclusive on request. In today's media scene, the ultimate success or credibility of a public relations person is to become one of those contacts who can frequently satisfy the hunger of particular reporters for exclusives. A note of caution, however. No public relations person can afford to oblige one particular reporter with exclusives consistently and ignore others. He should be equally ready to meet professional requests from all reporters.

C. Handouts

All Public Relations people remember that if a self-contained press release can be managed, there is no need to hold a press conference. A press conference is held only when a press release cannot encompass the whole gamut of news the organisation wants to release and when there is scope for further inquiries.

Preferably, a handout is prepared in such cases giving the salient points of the new development because of which the press conference is being held. The clever public relations person gives hints in his handout on what areas reporters can further explore through questions. He then introduces the person presiding — say the Chief Executive of his company — and invites him to address the reporters. But before this the public relations person is also to brief the Chief Executive on the focus of the press conference. The Chief Executive knows much more than the public relations person and much more than what the reporters would like to know. If he starts a harangue on the many achievements of his company, the reporters would yawn and some of them may go out thinking there could be better ways of utilising their time. It is the job of the public relations man to help the press conference get riveted to its focus. That is, it should relentlessly be aimed at the major news the organisation wants to break.

It must be noted that while all the juicy details come from the Chief Executive, the master of ceremonies is the public relations man. He must relentlessly try to focus the questioning on the area which is the field of achievement of the organisation — that is the achievement which is the provocation for holding this press conference. This he can do through informal hints to reporters, by drafting the Chief Executive's address in a way that they invite questions in the focus area, and of course by suitable hints in the handout.

One other reason for holding press conferences only when one has to is economy. Let us admit that the public relations budget of all organisations — including the biggest — is severely limited. This is indeed true of all budgets — demand is greater than supply. Hence a few press conferences meticulously prepared for, including hospitality and gifts if any, are far better than a large number of them in which the public relations man is struggling to control the expenditure of time, energy and money.

Beside the general briefing, the public relations man will do well to give to the Chief Executive the points listed in order of importance. It will be an even better idea if the public relations man has prepared slides or overhead projection transparencies and graphs to make the company's achievement and future plans come alive. It is good to remember that the more you value your company's achievement the more respect it will command from reporters.

D. Rejoinders

PR persons may sometimes be forced to be the front men in such public disputes. If that happens, they can perhaps not avoid it. But the golden rule is to stay clear of rejoinders, reposts or denials. The very simple reason is that by issuing rejoinders, reports or denials, the public relations person unwittingly gives public relations mileage to the other party. This is, first of all, not his job, and, secondly, by giving such mileage to the rival one dilutes the message he gives for his own organisation. A third reason is that by referring in a rejoinder or denial to something denigratory of one's organisation said by someone else, one is bringing it to the attention even of those who have not read the news to which it is a rejoinder. In the cases of those who have read the original denigratory news, the rejoinder serves to remind them that such a thing was originally said — and thus to reinforce the message. Sometimes, however, one has to react to negative news about one's organisation. In such cases, the clever public relations man would attempt to shift the focus from the negative news point to a positive one.

This brings us to a crucial issue. All dailies are not the same, just as all News Editors are not the same and all public relations persons are not the same. Dailies (or weeklies or fortnightlies) can be classified into two, three or four categories, specially in a metropolitan city like Delhi. There can be financial dailies, general purpose dailies or dailies which focus on particular regions or issues like sports. Accordingly, the intelligent public relations person will prepare two or three press releases or "rejoinders" for different categories of publications. "For each according to his need". Does it sound like throwing an extra, in some cases unbearable, burden on the public relations person? Specially as 99 per cent of the organisations—

government or private, political or economic — just prepare one press release and sprinkle it all over like salt being sprinkled on omelettes? No wonder 90 per cent or more of press releases land in the waste basket after the person concerned has read the first few words or the first sentence. Press releases, let us face it, are today treated with something bordering on contempt. Yet, the clever public relations man can indeed force News Editors to read his press releases beyond the first sentence and treat them with respect. This he can do by studying the needs of particular newspapers or particular classes of newspapers and tailor his press releases according to the needs of the particular paper or the particular class of newspapers. This brings us to two key formulations:

I. There is no such thing as a standard press release. Press releases must be tailored to the needs of particular newspapers or classes of newspapers.

II. The successful public relations person is not one who produces the largest number of press releases but one who produces press releases the largest percentage of which are used by newspapers (or periodicals).

E. Articles or Speeches

The foremost point to be said about writing articles is that the public relations person does not write them in his own name. He does not have the authority or the clout. He does write, but he is a ghost for the Chief Executive or the Finance Director, or whoever has the authority to speak on behalf of the organisation. This having been said (and, we hope, understood), here are some "dos" and "don'ts" about writing articles, it being assumed that the writing is done for publication and to fulfil a need.

1. The chef works for the eaters. Likewise, one writes

an article for the readers. Looks un-PR-like? Let us remember that a PR's job is to convey the message of the organisation to the reader, not to produdce a handout. If the message does not reach the reader, the entire effort is wasted. There is no public relations.

2. The writer's article carries his opinion or comment, just as the food is based on the chefs recipe. Yet both the food cooked and the article written should be relished by the consumers, otherwise they are wasted.
3. It is not necessary that every reader should become a convert for the article to be successful; it is enough if most readers appreciate the facts and arguments and the manner of their presentation.
4. To be relished by the reader, the opinion or the comment in the article should be plausible or convincing. To say that Mr Narasimha Rao is a bad man is not an article by itself; it can become an article if the writer marshals facts and arguments in proper sequence to show why he holds this opinion.
5. Yet another prerequisite for an article to be successful is that it should be topical. The reader would like to read about something that is exercising society's mind at the moment, not something forgotten or obscure.
6. If an article is intended to appeal to the reader, the writer should know — or visualise — the readership of the paper or journal in which it is meant to be published. An article on how scientists have improved the method of penicillin manufacture will be written differently for a professional journal

of drug manufacturers than if it were written for the *Statesman.* The vast majority of *Statesman* readers can be assumed not to know how penicillin is manufactured today. If the writer wants them to know of the improvement, he will have to tell them first how things are done today.

7. Another factor is that the article should be focussed on pushing one particular viewpoint. Every fact or argument that the writer knows or can find out should be marshalled. By the same token, things that are not relevant for projecting that viewpoint should be kept out because they dilute the force of the argument.
8. A factor which the article-writer must always bear in mind is that it is part of the mass communication process. That is, the readers of the journal should be able to understand what is being said. The article is wasted — even if the public relations man is able to persuade the News Editor to publish it — if it does not influence the reader. The objective is not merely to get the article published but to make it influence the reader.
9. Besides the above, there are two other major points which can decide the success or failure of an article. One, the article should have a fresh viewpoint to project, or at least advance fresh facts and arguments. If it says only that which other writers have been saying, it is a failure. The second factor is the placing of the article. So the article writer must study the needs of a magazine or newspaper. If he thinks a journal needs something like what he has in mind, he should proceed to write and send his article as fast as possible to the daily or periodical. .

7

Public Relations Advertising

The present age is purely materialistic. Public has grown as voracious mass consumer everywhere. Though economic prosperity is responsible for this. But mass awareness and education also played a lot for it. With the growth of consumerism and an increasing exposure of the common man to various media of communication, the organisations and the people who matter have to do a lot of explaining to their audience. Recently, a greater interdependence of public relations and advertising has been noticed. The organisations selling products have also felt the need to back up their products by promoting themselves in various positionings such as "market leader"; "blue chip company"; "company which attracts talents" and what have you. Public relations advertising known invariably as 'Corporate Advertising', 'Institutional Advertising', 'Public Service Advertising', serves as an important PR tool.

Basically, 'Advertising' is a paid communication that "attempts to inform and persuade a large number of people with a single communication." It presents a totally controllable message as the advertiser pays for the space or time subject to the law, the code of ethics etc. He also controls the frequency. Advertising delivers a message to a large number of people at low cost "per contact". On the other hand, in public relations, the message goes directly to the media through news releases and other means and is not paid for. It is, however, the prerogative of the news editor in the case of PR communication to accept or reject the news. That is why public relations news is sometimes referred to as "goodwill" communication. The output of public relations appears with uncontrolled frequency. These differences aside, advertising is increasingly being used by public relations practitioners as an important tool.

In fact, if public relations and advertising work in an integrated manner to create a total communication concept, the organisation can benefit in great way.

Public Relations and Advertising

Public relations as we agree influences public opinion; it creates an environment of acceptance with its persuasive skills. In the sixties and the seventies the developing countries with a population boom dreaded automation. The unions and the advocacy groups questioned the wisdom of governments bringing in automation and rendering the workforce idle. The IBM left India lock, stock and barrel as people were in no mood to switch on to computers. Not enough education was imparted about the use and usefulness of computers as an aid to human ingenuity and not a replacement. Today can we think of life without computers?

Basically, in the developed countries, the mean of literacy is changing. To be literate must also mean computer literate! For the success of a product, there has to be an environment of acceptance. Public relations has a definite role in this direction. Incidentally IBM is back in India, and so are many other international brands of computers. Another example which can be cited is the marketing of pressure cookers in the early seventies in our country. Till then, the average housewife thought that the longer the cooking period the tastier and more nutritious the meal.

In fact, the old generation had hesitation switching on to a gadget which would cook dishes in a jiffy! That the pressure cooker saved cooking time was not enough "value" for the buyer.

In the eighties of last century a number of cooking oils claiming low cholesterol entered the market. The "unique selling proposition" (USP) was good health, especially a fight against thickening arteries and heart problems. No advertising could have prepared the ground as well as public relations had done by influencing the opinion of consumers, whose action in buying the product seemed voluntary, though stimulated. Using public relations before formally launching a product in the market place proved the winning strategy.

With the consumer movement picking up all over and the legislation in many countries protecting consumer rights, the tall claims by advertising have at times earned the ire of consumer groups. The issues no more seem fit for advertising, they seem to change to public relations issues. The battle may be won or lost through legal means, but the ultimate deciding factor is the consumer.

Public Relations Advertising

In crisis situations specially, when a company is not able to get full coverage for its point of view, it may buy space and time to reach out to the constituent publics with full facts. Public relations practitioners at times resort to paid advertising when their more traditional means of communication do not promise to achieve their objective and they need a quick, direct and widely disseminated form of communication. When there is more than one party involved, say an industrial relations tangle like an imminent lockout situation or threat of strike fay unions, many companies have used advertising to give their part of the message through paid advertising, on which they had full control.

In the present time of advance information technology as Public Relations practitioners we have to realise that we have to be ready, should such eventualities take place.

Public Relations-based advertisements are different from regular advertising in that they consist of copy with little or no pictorial/graphic support. They generally are copy-heavy compared to the average ad. The language is also simple, concise and straightforward to inform or educate and not necessarily to stimulate for action.On the other hand institutional or corporate advertising combines public relations and advertising, in which image and goodwill are sold against a specific product or service. According to Ronald P Lovell (*Inside Public Relations*) "a corporation decides to use institutional advertising for many reasons such as to create goodwill, to counteract adverse press comment, to make known its public position on an important issue, to inform the public about its products and employees, to educate the public about an industry or an issue. Usually the action desired is less immediate and concrete than in the straight PR advertisements".

Corporate advertising can have a number of objectives like: (a) to give "added value" to the products of the company, (b) to encourage people to trust and enjoy dealing with the company.

According to Tob Garbett, "Corporate advertising is not product advertising. It is not classified or mail-order advertising and it usually is not retail advertising".

US-based Leading National Advertisers (LNA), a group charged with reading and tabulating ads in America's top magazines and select newspapers, have a standard definition: "To truly be labelled 'corporate' the ad must deal with the company's policies, functions, facilities, objectives, ideas, and standards, build favourable opinions of the company's management, skill, technology, or social contributions, enhance the investment qualities or financial structure of the company or promote it as a good place to work."

Remarkably in the recent past, the line between corporate and product ads has become finer than ever. Product ads have taken on a distinctly "corporate" look, and corporate ads are being used to push products. Classifying the ads has become a trying task. Kathy Burke is of opinion that ads in general are looking more editorial. And "teaser" and "image" ads, difficult to clarify at any time, are now the rage. "Determining which is which can sometimes be as difficult as telling a crocodile from an alligator", she wonders. One of the advertisements which can fit in this category is a double-page colour ad by Kelvinator with the headline "wanted a person with the following qualifications to design India's largest single-door fridge" (*A&M*, April 1993). The idea is obviously not to recruit a technologist but to get consumers to know the company is planning to put in the market "India's largest single-door fridge."

With more and more companies going "public", it has become almost customary to launch a corporate campaign as a prelude to financial advertising. Corporate campaigns are designed to woo prospective shareholders by giving them an insight into the company's working and its distinct market position. While resorting to corporate advertising, a company can speak of its achievements, how it has created a niche for itself, and its contribution to society in any specific area. Sometimes industries take up social or national causes without even a mention of their product or services except giving their corporate identity — a byline or a logo. Such ads are also referred to as "public service ads".

Selling a product with some percentage of exaggeration seems all right because the buyer takes ads with a pinch of salt, but when a company projects its beliefs and convictions it has to stand up for them. As per some expert opinion, it has become fashionable these days to launch institutional campaigns even when there is no need. To cite the advice of Ronald P. Lovell is very ope to in this connection who says— "Such campaigns are expensive, and even a wealthy company cannot afford to waste its resources". Hence, it is advisable, he says, that after an institutional campaign gets going, its effectiveness should be evaluated periodically.

To conclude, Corporate advertising in modern times has come up in big way—most aggressive, boastful, may be with only partial tinge of truth. Due to low level of public awareness (though some improved in comparison to recent past decade) they sometimes prove misguiding. Laxity and recklessness on the part of regulatory authority (or even in lack of it) ethical code of conduct is never followed. The real demand of the time is be competitive, ethical, qualitative and truth-oriented—in advertising. Facts are facts. Reap fruits now and for long run.

REFERENCES

1. John, Wilmshurst, *The Fundamentals of Advertising.*
2. Tom Garbett, *Corporate Advertising*—the what, the why and how.
3. Merlye Davids and Michael Winklemn, "Blurred Vision," *PR Journal,* September, 1987.

8

Public Relations with Internal Publics

The internal publics of an organisation are part of that core group which has very intimate relationship and a stake in the company. By virtue of their closeness to the company, they have direct access to all types of information about the company. Therefore, it is essential that company in order to win their confidence, loyality and goodwill takes care of their needs, expectations and suggestions. Indifferent attitude or lukewarm approach towards them exposes company to a very vulnerable situation where it might not only lose its credibility in the eyes of its customers, government, press and general public, but it also might lose its business secrets, technology and future plans. So far most of the Indian companies have not accepted these internal publics consisting of investors, employees, suppliers, distributors, dealers, retailers, management consultants, lawyers, solicitors, advertising agencies, auditors etc., as their business partners and have exploited them for fulfilment of their business purposes.

For sustaining and strengthening this relationship with the passage of time and growth of the company, it is essential that company should design special communication channels with each one of them keeping in mind their needs, objectives of communication, regularity of feedback and seeking their participation and cooperation by allocating an appropriate budget and employees to ensure that it continues on a continuing basis.

Internal Publics

A public is any group that has an actual or potential interest in or impact on an organisation's ability to achieve its objectives. Depending upon the interest or the impact it exercises on the organisation, it influences and affects its functioning accordingly. These include shareholders who own the company, the employees who run the company and carry out the decisions of the management to take it to its goals, suppliers who provide raw material to the company without which it is not possible for the company to produce any product or to provide any services, distributors who carry the product or the services of the company to the retailer or to the end-user and the retailer who is the last link in the chain and who is the representative of the company not only as a salesperson but also as public relations representative. Each one of them is extremely important for the functioning of the company and has a special stake in it either in terms of their investment business interest or career prospects. Their interest in the company is of varying order and may not be always complementary to each other. They can be classified in the following categories:

1. *Employees:* Employees are also part of the internal publics of an organisation. It is through them that a company fulfils its objectives. It needs their cooperation and understanding on a continuous basis in all its activities including the public relations activities. If a company is able to communicate effectively with its employees and seek their participation and cooperation, they can act as the best public relations agents of the company while dealing with their friends, relations, neighbours and business associates. Such active and conscious role on their part will also reduce the number of complaints, grievances and provide much better services to various external publics.

The psychology of an employee is entirely different when he comes to work.

He becomes a unique combination of business and non-business qualities of a person. Among other things, the pressure of their own work group is most predominent in their behaviour and attitude towards company, their superiors and the work itself. They can be characterised into executive, supervisory, non-supervisory and unskilled employees. Executives normally belong to non-unionised category of employees, but they are also getting unionised in many public and private sector undertakings.

2. *Investors:* A investor is the one who has financial stake in the company. He provides finances to the company either as a shareholder or as a long-term or short-term creditor. He may have a fixed return on his investment or it may vary depending on the financial performance of the company. If he becomes the shareholder, he becomes the owner of the company who gets dividend, rights shares, bonus shares, discount coupons for purchase of companies' products or concessional usage of its services and gifts on special occasions like annual conference, anniversary celebration etc. Debentureholders include convertible and non-convertible debenrureholders. Their financial involvement in the company is for the limited period depending upon the maturity period of their debentures.

3. *Distributors:* Distributors are perform the important task of merchandising the products of the company from one place to another by ensuring its safe and timely delivery to the retailers/dealers of the company. They are either given a fixed percentage as the commission or they are allowed to sell the product at the flexible price ensuring a reasonable profit margin for themselves. They operate on the business principle of high turnover and low margin

and the high turnover of the transaction ensures a reasonable profit for them.

4. *Suppliers:* Supplier can be defined as the one who provides raw material to the company. The raw material is processed by the company depending upon its technology and converted into finished product Company sells these finished products at a higher price than the cost of raw material and thus earns profit. He has to supply the right quality of material in the right quantity at a right place and at a right time to ensure regular supply of finished goods to the customers and enable the company to earn sufficient profits so that it can make provision for future expansion and diversification. His association with the company may not be always convenient and profitable for him as company normally selects their suppliers on the basis of annual tenders. He has to absorb the fluctuations in the market price of the raw material himself to keep up his promise. A good company cannot be happy if its suppliers are not happy because they are its business associates and they are also in business to make profit.

5. *Other Business Associates:* Apart from above mentioned business associates, a company has lot of other business associates who have intimate knowledge of the performance of the company and who regularly provide their untiring support and cooperation to the company. They include promoters, friends and relations of the directors of the company, chartered accountants who are part of statutory audit, government auditors, consultants, lawyers and advisers of the company who may be engaged on a regular basis or on occasional basis. They may not be in forefront of the company but their role and influence on the working of the company cannot be undermined under any circumstances.

6. Retailers and Dealers: The retailers and dealers are the one who ultimately deliver the goods to the consumers for fulfilment of their needs. Consumer perceives them as company because they are the only visible part of the company to the consumer. Thus, they make complaints, bring their grievances and give suggestions to improve the product and performance of the company. In order to live up to the expectations of its customers, it is very essential that retailer and dealer should be encouraged with conducive environment to pass on the feedback to the company. Good companies, therefore, organise annual conferences of their dealers which are normally attended by the entire top management of the company to ensure prompt corrective action on the feedback received from the dealers.

Significance of Internal Publics

It is very essential that the public relations department should take preemptive action specially while dealing with internal publics, although it is also desirable while dealing with external publics. The so-called corrective action many a time proves to be crying over split milk. Internal publics by virtue of their proximity and intimate relationship with the company, have access to all types of confidential, sensitive and secret information about the business, functioning and problems of the company. In event of any clash of interest or conflict, there is every likelihood that any of the internal publics may prove harmful and even fatal for the business interest and the corporate image of the company. Another factor which has to be kept in mind while dealing with them is that they are a means through which the objectives of the business and the company are to be achieved.

Therefore, they should always have major share in the

growth and prosperity of the company and their views and suggestions should always be looked into very seriously to make better use of their knowledge, skill, performance and potential.

Relations with Internal Publics

It is to be noted, public relations professionals have never spent so much of their time and energy in sustaining their relationship with internal publics as they have to spend now in view of their growing demands. Dealing with new demands and challenges from employees' organisations, shareholders uniting themselves under the banner of Investors' forums and minutely analysing each and every decision of the Board of Directors have made annual general meeting a very unpredictable affair these days.

2. *Employees Relations:* The basic difference of opinion with management is recognition of their right to be respected and treated in a decent way. What the employees look for now is not only salary, but achieving fulfilment of their higher needs of ego and esteem, love and affiliation and self-actualisation. How these needs are to be fulfilled at the work place and away from work are throwing new challenges for personnel and public relations professionals. The leadership and management styles of our executives, their vales, attitudinal profile, all have to undergo a sea-change in order to effectively deal with the situation.

1. *Shareholders Relations:* Shareholder is the legal owner of the company but unfortunately he has been treated in a shabby manner by most of the companies. Mainly it is because of his financial investment and risk that company has come into existence and thereafter if his contribution is not recognised and appreciated, obviously he will feel aggrieved and annoyed. Whether it is transfer of shares,

or change of address or non-receipt of dividend or annual report, there seems to be no easy hearing even for his genuine grievances. The only function seems to be performed by public relations professionals in such cases, is a rebuttal or quick requital after the complaint appears in newspapers. Acknowledgement of mistake or lapse will be the first honest and sincere effort on their part to put the foundation of good relations with them in such cases.

4. Suppliers Relations: Generally, 'Company' prefers to deal with known suppliers and therefore makes such request to them rather than dealing with a new supplier. Suppliers do accommodate such requests from company in anticipation of nurturing harmonious relationship with the company. Suppliers need the company and company needs the supplier. It is the mutuality of purpose which keeps them together. When the good gesture of supplier to the company is not responded with an equally good gesture, there is a likelihood of their relations getting strained. The normal causes for straining the relationship is non-payment or undue delay in payment of suppliers' bills, high amount of rejection of raw material supplied by them, uncareful treatment by any department of the company etc.

5. Distributors/Dealers Relations: To strengthen its relationship with its distributors, dealers and retailers, companies design special communications for them from time to time, announce various prise schemes, discount schemes and provide them incentives both monetary and non-monetary in nature. Merit certificates, performance certificates and certificates of good work done are granted by the company at special functions held for this purpose.

6. Other Associate Relations: Management consultants, lawyers, solicitors, auditors etc., who form this core group of special internal publics of an organisation, are to be always remembered and cared by the company; special mention about their contribution in the annual report at the annual general meeting of the company, special functions organised by the company on the occasion of its anniversary, special achievement etc., and sending them special invitation for all the important functions of the company, is part of good public relations with them. Similarly copies of company publications, annual reports, new issues, preferential issues etc., should be regularly sent to them to give them special feeling that they matter to the company and they are eligible for these privileges because of their association with the company. Congratulatory letters or greetings on their birthdays, marriage anniversaries or special achievements put company into a category of special groups who have an easy access to them.

Summing Up

The internal publics are becoming more demanding and aware about its own rights and asking for the status of a business associate rather than that of only a means of production. The employees of the company at all levels are the best public relations agents of the company. If they are looked after nicely and kept in high morale, they serve other groups of internal publics with sincerity and dedication. The relationship between employees, shareholders, debentureholders, depositors, suppliers, distributors, dealers, retailers and other business associates and the company have a mutuality of interest. Till a time, they keep on responding positively to each others' needs and expectations, the relationship bond will remain cordial and strengthened.

REFERENCES

Alien Fred T., *Ways to Improve Employee Communication,* National Business, September, 1975, pp. 54-56.

Bateman J. Carroll, *Public Relations for Business and Professional Association.*

D.M. Silvera, *Human Resource Development, The Indian Experience,* News India Publication, 1988, New Delhi.

Fraser P. Seitel, Charles E., *The Practice of Public Relations,* Merrill Publishing Co, A Bell & Howell Company, Columbus, Ohio.

Zausner M., *Corporate Policy and Investment Community,* New York, Ronald Press, 1968.

9

Media Planning

Generally publicity, advertising, periodicals, films, special events and oral communications etc. are the major communication media used by different organisations for public relations. The most widely used is media publicity in the form of news releases, feature stories, magazine articles, photographs, audio and video tapes and films. Successful Public Relations do much to improve an organisation's potential for projecting a desired image. The Public Relations officer should take care to see that the message is timely and projected thus making the purchase of time and space to the optimum use. Hence advertising becomes a significant tool of Public Relations.

Media Relations

Here also the news media constitute a major factor in public relations, controlling the flow of publicity through the most important channels of public communication. Good working relations with the editors, reporters, broadcasters, cameraman etc., are essential in securing good publicity coverage. With the increasing number of media and its specilisation, competition for space and time has intensified and publicity has attained a more significant role in Public Relations. As Public Relations practitioners have become more professional in their approach to publicity, they develop a community of interest with news writers. Editors are recognising that Public Relations departments are a source of genuine news and technical information. On the other hand, Public Relations professionals are acquiring a better knowledge of mass media and operating problems.

Media Selection

Accuracy in selection of the mass media is essential in preparing and placing news releases for achieving successful results. The common practice of indiscriminate mailing of releases and articles is wasteful. Considering the high cost and the excessive waste in worthless releases, the preparation and distribution of publicity must be given greater attention by publicity departments. Systematic collection of information about the audiences and editorial requirements of newspapers, magazines and radio and television stations is also essential in reducing the waste.

Newspapers and magazines should be read and broadcasts audited to determine the publicity they use. Editors may be asked for sample copies of their publications for review. Editors may be interviewed at their offices, invited to lunch and tactfully tackled about their editorial policy. Records should be maintained of all periodicals sent for an analysis about the effectiveness of the publicity.

There are different types of publicity media available.

Magazines: Magazines are an important medium for product news, feature stories and pictorial publicity. They tend to be read leisurely and thoroughly. In some cases, magazines may be preserved for future reference. The attractive appearance, quality paper and fine colour reproduction of magazines make them ideal for picture publicity.

Newspapers: Newspapers are the major medium of publicity. They are read by millions, enjoy reader confidence, influence public opinion, appear regularly and intensively cover local and regional areas. Newspapers appeal to the special interests of business executives, women, sports enthusiasts and others through special sections providing opportunities for product publicity on these subjects.

Radio and Television: Radio and TV publicity has developed rapidly. In this age of science, there can only be a few areas which do not come under the network system of TV/Radio. It is a powerful media and a believable news source.

Public Relations Operation Techniques

The main tool of Public Relations is communication. This sounds simple enough but the kind of communication carried on is not the spontaneous communication that takes place when people just sit down and talk to each other. It is purposeful communication that is intended for to change people's attitudes, to motivate them to certain kinds of action. In the hands of those who know how to use this tool effectively it can become a very powerful instrument indeed, and sometimes Public Relations men have been under fire because some unscrupulous people amongst them have used this instrument to achieve ends that were not socially desirable. But Public Relations in the true sense of the term involves an identification of the particular interest with the social or public interest.

Communications

Communication though it may seem to be a simple phenomena, as a tool of public relations we conceive of communications as a purposeful and organised system intended to achieve certain objectives. It is only when we are able to understand all that the process of communication involves that we will be able to make use of this tool for our own purpose.

The communication process involves the conception and the sending of the message. It requires an instrument for the conveying of the message which may be the human voice or some other written, printed, visual or audio visual media. It presupposes also the existence of a receiver of the message. The process can only be said to be complete when the receiver of the message has comprehended the meaning of the message sent. It is, therefore, necessary that the language and the medium of the message should be capable of being understood by the person who receives the message. Unless, therefore, this whole process of conceiving, sending, receiving and comprehending a message is completed, effective communication cannot be said to have taken place. The communications may be of two kinds External and Internal.

External communications are with the financiers, government and parliament, press, dealers and community while internal communications are within the organisations. The difference between a well managed industry and a poorly managed turn out to be a reflection of the sort of communications system operating in them. But it is given a low priority. It is generally supposed that the kind of communication that has evolved spontaneously in the organisation is the best that could be thought of or in any case adequate for the purpose.

Communication Media

The communication media can be divided under three heads. Audio or oral representing those media of communication which are by word of mouth and the visual which includes written, pictorial and symbolic media as well as combinations of both.

House Journals: As a popular mode the house journal, if properly planned, edited and distributed, the most effective medium of communication. The house journal may also be designed for external projection of an organisation or to communicate with dealers, suppliers or other publics. It has got to have the professional approach in its format, periodicity, gathering news, editing, photographs, layout, contents etc.

Advertising: Advertising is a major Public Relations tool used to communicate with both internal and external publics. It has its primary objective of projecting the company as an institution interested in society's welfare as well as to create a favourable public image. Public Relations advertising is used to promote public welfare.. For an advertisement to be aimed at public good, it has to fulfil the following criteria:

1. It must build favourable opinion about the company by stressing the competence of the company's management, the company's accumulated knowledge, manufacturing skills, technological progress and product improvements and its contribution to social advancement.
2. Advertising must educate, inform or impress the public regarding the company's policies, style of functioning facilities, objectives, ideals and standards.
3. Advertising must 'sell' the company as a good place to work with.

Public Relations advertising is an effective medium of communication. It is economical since it can transmit Public Relations messages to a varied audiences at a relatively low cost. It can be highly selective and concentrated on a particular segment of public. Instant communication is possible through daily newspapers. Intensive local coverage may be secured through newspapers, radio, broadcast.

Principles and Objectives of Public Relations Advertising

1. Misconceptions Rectification

Misunderstandings may seriously affect the sales and profit of the company or the financial support or voluntary aid and so on. Advertisements are used to comet misconceptions by publishing facts about their policies and practices to the public.

2. Favourable Image Creation

PR advertising is used to enhance public confidence in it and its product and services. A company that can create a favourable public attitude can aspire to sell more of its products and services thereby building a loyal dealer organisation.

3. Securing Good Suppliers

An increasing number of manufacturers and merchants advertise in selling their product to the manufacturers and merchants to invite suppliers to 'open houses' and to promote the welfare of resources.

4. Goodwill Winning of Neighbouring Community

Institutional advertising is a part of corporate Public Relations programme. They tell the community about the operations of the firm and its contribution to the welfare of the community. This also highlights the company's role in creating jobs and employment.

5. Creating Interest of Stockholders and Financial Community

Corporations advertise in the financial sections of newspapers and in financial magazines to inform shareholders and the financial community about their financial condition.

6. Informing Government Officials

Advertisement is discussing issues involved in pending legislation and to seek the support of the government.

7. Earning Goodwill of the Employees

Basically, local newspapers, broadcast and employee magazines are utilised to inform workers about the company, policies, plans accomplishments and future programmes. They are helpful to dispel rumours and create a better climate.

8. Developing Goodwill of Dealers

Generally trade magazines and mail advertising is used by manufacturers to present their policies, promotions and developments. Advertising in trade publications is also used to guide merchants in better and effective merchandising and promotion of sales.

9. Consumers Service

Broadly, consumer magazines, radio and TV reach consumers with information about the company's contribution to public welfare. They help consumers solving problems of contemporary mundane life such as pollution, traffic safety and inflation, etc.

10. Rendering Public Service

Advertising is highly used by corporations to promote highway safety, national health and charitable work.

11. Ameliorating Labour Relations

PR advertising in local newspapers is used to keep employees and community informed about benefits, working conditions and labour policy. It is also used to present management's position in a labour dispute and to dispel misunderstanding of its motives.

Research and Evaluation

The fact-finding is the ultimate aim of any Public Relations programme or strategy. While knowledge of the basic principles of Public Relations is an essential prerequicite for the development of Public Relations programmes, it is necessary to appreciate that there is no readymade formula that will apply to all situations. In developing and executing a Public Relations programme for any organisation one must try to study the specific situation in the context of which the programme has to be developed. When applying Public Relations to any organisation, there is need to work out a strategy for the long term as well as for the short term achievement of results.

Hence Public Relations is waging a war to change people's attitudes, overcome prejudices, suspicions and dislikes and establish instead goodwill and understanding. For success and result-orientation, a Public Relations programme will have to proceed through four stages: (a) Fact finding ; (b) Planning; (c) Implementationl and Evaluation.

(a) Sources from which facts may be gleaned are press reports and comments, proceedings of the Central Parliament of State Legislatures, reports of customer reactions obtained from the company's own sale force or from dealers and distributors, employees comments, the kind of response the company gets when it puts out an advertisement for recruitment. In most cases these will add up to give a fairly clear picture of the kind of image the organisation has, of its weaknesses and strengths.

(b) In planning, the strategy various steps that are needed to be taken should be carefully studied. The means of communication to be adopted, an estimation of costs, requirements of manpower etc. are some factors to be given proper thought of. In all cases, even where the Public Relations man has been authorises to prepare and execute his plans within the frame work of an overall budget, it is desirable to keep top management informed to try to secure their cooperation in the implementation of the plan.

(c) Similarly in the implementation of the Public Relations programmes, the definite target audience and media or other media required to influence the people should be examined. With the precise definition of the audience, the message is likely to get diffused and considerable waste involved.

(d) An evaluation has to be made to knew how far the objectives have been achieved. It may be necessary where there is some doubt or controversy with regard to the results to take recourse to the process of formal research. Having found out the results and the extent to which the objectives originally set have been achieved, the person man will move to launch the next one.

Therefore, there is, a main theme of Public Relations programme, being the investigation of facts of the situation, a study of what the problem is and what is involved in an effort to tackle the problem. Systematic fact finding will eliminate all prevailing uncertainties. It is necessary to assemble a basic fact file or each case and to operate continuous intelligency activities constantly adding to the basic fact file.

Definitely, there are limitations of research. The findings of research are only meant to provide data to help in decision making. It is not something to be used everywhere in all kinds of situations. Knowing when to use research and how to make use of research is something that requires skill and experience. It has to be remembered that the findings of research are only part of the total informations mix that is required for the planning of Public Relations strategy. Research can help point to the management to get an insight into the reasons when certain attitudes develop or change or do not develop.

Effectiveness of Public Relations Campaign Evaluation

Results relative to disciplines like Marketing. Marketing Research, Sales Management and Advertising Operations are tangible as they can be analysed and recorded in arithmetical terms. Such is not the case with Public Relations as the result produced by it is intangible.

Public Relations in Management

A big difference between managing and doing is there. How successful is one in one's managerial practice lies in how well could one understand 'managing and 'doing' and go about his duties accordingly; and that is the core of Public Relations in Manager Statesmanship.' The manager often finds himself in the position of the interplanetary traveller who doesn't know how fast he is going unite he knows where he is and can't know where he is until he knows how fast he is keeping pace with his activities. Often the result is that the manager knows that he may have to take refuge in spending most of his time dealing with that which makes his most secure, and administrative problem-solving. In other words, he relies more on doing than managing Not that 'doing' ins't important. In fact, a manager's doing activities may become more important than his managing activities especially if he has only a couple of subordinates. But there has to be a point where managing activity gets the attention it needs.

How much the result is based on status and how much on reason or emotional adherence is not always determinable. The manager who has had some insight into public relations knows about the efficiency of using 'orders' depending upon situations. Examples are:

Guidelines

1. When to "Request"
   (a) To the touchy or sensitive worker
   (b) To the untrained worker
   (c) To the nervous, irritable worker
   (d) To get a little more done
   (e) To the man who is interested in his work
   (f) To a person of equal footing
   (g) first time you reprimand or caution a worker
   (h) To avoid making a man sore
   (i) To an older man-in age and service
   (j) To the "hard-boiled" man
   (k) To do a difficult job in a particular way.

1. When to' 'Command"
   (a) In case of danger
   (b) For the lazy and indifferent worker
   (c) To the careless man
   (d) When the workman refuses to obey safely orders and rules
   (e) To the agitator
   (f) To the workman who refuses to do the work as he is told
   (g) To stop waste or delay
   (h) To the disobedient worker.

3. When to "Suggest"—for fully experienced workers
   (a) When improved methods are sought
   (b) To the man who is trying to get ahead

(c) To the man who is trying to assume responsibility

(d) Try it out with a new group of experienced workmen

(e) Use it to develop initiative.

Empathy

What is empathy? Webster opines it is Imaginative projection of one's own consciousness in another being. In advertising, then it is the Agency representative's it is seeing matters as others see them. It is the executive causing himself to feel as others feel, and even his feelings for them. The empathic executive treats each client in a considerate manner. His capacity for empathy permits the executive to be sympathetic to the client's attitudes and beliefs, sensitive to the client's hopes and fears, receptive to the client's ideas and reactions, and appreciative of the client's objectives and values. When empathy is operating, the Public Relations executive thinks in terms of his 'publics', not just himself. He gives his client no impression of conceit, superiority, condecension, criticism, irritation or impatience. Instead his sincere question is "How can I help the client get what he wants most?" Being an empathic executive is an art—it is an ability a Public Relations executive must acquire and master if he is to realise his full potential. This takes time, planned practice, experimentation and experience. A Public Relations executive should want to perfect his skill in this area until his attempts to understand each of his publics' automatic.

Remember! Empathy contributes to a Public Relations executive's success in several ways. It helps making client's relationship better. It fosters greater understanding. Empathy tells an executive when he should be firm and when he should be more restrained when he should talk

2nd when he should remain salient, even whether he should joke or be serious. The empathic Public Relations executive is more accurate than the non-empathic competitor in interpreting what a client/buyer says or does. Empathy encourages the client to be frank and sincere with the Public Relations executive, or reveal, instead of conceal. It encourages the client to welcome and even to look forward to subsequent visits with the Public Relations executive.

Evolution of Ethical Standards in Public Relations

Standards of business conduct, as all ethical standards have their geneses largely in the moral codes of the religious doctrines which are accepted by the particular society. This tends to act as a unifying force toward acceptance of given moral concepts by a majority of the citizens of the society. Nonetheless, since the answer to any question of morality hinges in the relative and qualitative criteria of "right" and "wrong" the problem of what constitutes proper business and professional conduct is controversial.

Before the dawn of the last century (i.e. 20th century), a discernible change began to occur in the social and economic forces which so strongly influence public opinion of "right" and "wrong". Standards of morality were viewed with a new objectivity, possibly due to the complexity of the developing professions arising from industrial, social and political as well as constraints and the attendant distance between professionals and their clients. Or perhaps the tremendous increase in the numbers of people practising various professions.

Whatever the responsible forces, the fact is that the void between man's three sets of moral standards -his treatment of other people, the treatment he expects others to accord him, and the manner that he thinks others people should treat each other - began to close, and more objective view of standards is in ample evidence. This transition did not result from an overnight conversion of the population to "higher thought", but as with all changes involving people, was a gradual shift to meet the irresistible demands of both economic and social changes. What then is meant by the term "ethical standards of conduct in profession"? Various authorities seem to be in fair agreement as to the general meaning of the term "ethics".

(1) In every field except ethics all kinds of professionals are concerned primarily with things as they are. In ethics, however, they are concerned with things as they ought to be for themselves and their clients.

(2) Ethics, the study of moral principles and conduct: Truth is absolute, but ethical standards are relative; they exist to meet the practical needs of people in varying situations and circumstances.

(3) Ethics, or moral responsibility, as it is sometimes called, consists of a body of social laws and theories that has grown and evolved through the ages from as far back in history as man has recorded life.

(4) Ethics deals with personal conduct and moral duty and concerns human relations with respect to right and wrong."

(5) Ethics is the science of conduct. But by no means all of conduct concerns us in a study of Ethics. Clearly a large part of our conduct is without ethical significance-neither good nor bad, right nor wrong, moral nor immoral, except as special conditions may affect the action or its results.

A careful overview of the above statements can lead us to evolve a definition of ethics that would include the concept that ethics is a code, or set of rules, that determines the degree of lightness of conduct involving oneself, oneself and another person or another group of person. The use of the ethics code as a measuring device is inherent within the definition and meaning of ethics. The pragmatic application is at once obvious. If the results of a person's conduct are beneficial, good, or at least innocuous, then the conduct is right or ethical. However, the intent a motivating the person conducting himself in a given manner should also be measured. If one intended the results of his conduct to be beneficial or good, then the conduct is right or ethical.

To our utter dinay as in the present time, good results are the fruit of evil intentions and complete fiascos result from the best of inventions; therefore, neither measurement can be used to the exclusion of the other. In today's dynamic world of management, where time for meditating upon the intents of one's conduct is crowded out by the necessity of deciding what future conduct is to be undertaken, only the results of a persons's actions are usually measured in determining if conduct is ethical or not.

10

Public Relations Education

With the growing demand of public relations professionals in Government, public and private sectors, the need of public relations education is being felt. Consequent upon this some institutions have started Diploma/Degree courses.

Although public relations has been in practice for over half a century and although courses in public relations are being run in universities and colleges in many countries, there was until recently little attempt at coordination. The need was, however, felt to achieve some harmonising of educational standards. For this purpose, the International Public Relations Association (IPRA) decided in 1980 that the time was opportune for a systematic study of the state of public relations education as it existed in different countries and to make recommendations for public relations education and for professional standards and practice in this field. The Report and the Working Group of IPRA recommendations were published in January 1982.

The Chairman of the IPRA Education and Research Committee in his introduction to the Paper stated "In considering the elements of public relations education it is essential always to respect the individual nature of a country's culture and historical background. .The theory of public relations is valid everywhere but its practical application must take, into account national character, economy and environment. IPRA's role, as exemplified by the production of this Gold Paper, is to synthesise the experience of different countries and to encourage national public relations associations to adapt the best examples; from other countries to the formation of national, public relations educational and professional advancement programmes best suited to their milieu".

Despite having been taught as a discipline at many universities since 1923, public relations is still developing its full potential. Like the practice itself, public relations education has not adequately been defined. In their view, public relations education consists of not just public relations courses, but of study in all disciplines linked through a common communication core. They also express the belief that those who intend to study public relations at universities should first obtain a general liberal education. Ideally, therefore, public relations education should be provided mainly for those students who have received, a first university degree in other fields, such as, commerce, sociology, psychology and journalism.

Examining the question of what is expected from the public relations function, the IPRA Commission expresses the following views:

Professional public relations operates in every sphere of life:

1. Government—national, regional, local and international.
2. Business and Industry—small, medium and transnational.
3. Community and Social Affairs.
4. Educational Institutions, Universities, Colleges, etc.
5. Hospitals and Health Care.

6. Charities and good causes.
7. International Affairs.

Public relations practice is:

1. Counselling based on an understanding of human behaviour
2. Analysing future trends and predicting; their consequences.
3. Research into public opinion, attitudes and expectations and advising on necessary action.
4. Establishing and maintaining two-way, communication based on truth and full information.
5. Preventing conflict and misunderstandings.
6. Promoting mutual respect and social responsibility.
7. Harmonising the private and the public interest.
8. Promoting good-will with staff, suppliers and customers.
9. Improving industrial relations.
10. Attracting good personnel and reducing labour turn over.
11. Promotion of products or services.
12. Maximising profitability.
13. Projecting a corporate identity.
14. Encouraging an interest in international affairs.
15. Promoting an understanding of democracy.

A typical public relations activity will have four parts

1. Analysis, research and defining problems.
2. Drawing up a programme of action.
3. Communicating and implementing the programme.
4. Monitoring the results, evaluation and possible modification.

Again, the Paper also points out that whereas previously top management spent some 80% of their time managing their organisation, possibly 10% communicating and the remainder at leisure, now the proportions are changing as communications are becoming so demanding. Discussing its implications, the Paper states:

> To public relations managers this implies that their future depends on staying ahead of senior management's needs; they must keep looking at the next area of concern, translating today's issues of concern into future opportunities by injecting this knowledge into corporate policy consistent with public opinion and translating it into public relations programmes of action.
>
> Today, public opinion today may be sceptical of authority and more discerning but it seeks more-management not less, not just more care over sales and profits but also over natural and human resources, i.e., more concern about environmental pollution and conservation consumer health and employee safety. People want more disclosure of financial data, closer finks between the private and public sectors, and greater fairness in the use of the free market. People want access to information so that they can ask 'why' and 'why not' and so they can participate.
>
> Public relations practitioners are the eyes and ears of management. They should be able to coordinate with other functions: law, finance, marketing and personnel, and to produce the most cost-effective communication methods of reaching the various audiences.
>
> Our challenge is to switch from being reactive to being proactive; from peripheral to central decision-making; from tactical to strategic advisers. The role of public relations as detector, evaluator, interpreter and communicator becomes ever more important with the growth of more groups and institutions representing different interests across the world. Dealing with this diversity of people and interests demands great skills and sophistication, and growing specialisation increases

> the need for broad understanding—to be generalists in the age of specialists.
>
> The ability to comprehend the overall business strategy, the corporate policy, the market place, the external environment, is vital.
>
> Public relations will either become recognised as indispensable to the vitality of all organisations or it will be relegated to merely carrying out a useful range of techniques. All public relations education needs both a solid base in scientific approach and a society-oriented, forward-aiming emphasis. Only such a combination will produce students of public relations capable of filling, professional jobs at management level.

The Gold Paper then takes up the question of research. It is pointed out that research is of two types—(1) pure and basic research and (2) applied research. In this connection, some examples of research subjects that have been cited are:

1. Communications—network research.
2. System—theory research, applied to practical planning and public relations strategy.
3. Environmental analysis research.
4. Attitude and image research.
5. Effects—evaluation research.
6. Operation research, (decision research).
7. Prevention analysis.
8. Crisis management research.
9. Models for pre and post-test techniques.
10. Mediating factors research in information flow.
11. Fundamental research.

Whereas relatively little has been done in the field of basic or pure research, a certain amount of research work is being done, both to obtain information that can be used for public relations planning and programme development purposes and to try to measure and evaluate the effectiveness of some of the work being done in the field. This leads on to the question of trying to evaluate accurately the effectiveness of work in public relations. Unless some methods are found of objectively establishing the results of public relations activity, it will fail to achieve the credibility that is needed if it is to establish itself as one of the management sciences.

It is a difficult taks to measure the effectiveness of public relations programmes because it is often difficult to isolate the results of public relations activity from environmental or other effects. Where, however, specific objectives have been clearly defined, it should be possible to measure reasonably accurately whether these objectives have been realised partially or fully.

The following are some of the methods used to measure the effectiveness of public relations programmes.

1. Benchmark Surveys and Communications Audits.
2. Media quality and quantity assessment.
3. Periodic management reviews
4. Perception research.
5. Supplier and customer interrogation.
6. Government reaction.
7. Environmental monitoring.

The recommendations finally given by the IPRA Commission in its Gold paper have been summed up as follows:

1. Ideally, public relations full-time education should be offered in universities at second degree (Masters)

level. It must be accepted, however, that for the time being most education will continue to be given to young undergraduates taking first degrees (Bachelor's degrees).

2. Public relations should by preference be taught as a social science with both academic and professional emphasis.
3. Public relations courses should be taught by individuals with a sound experience and understanding of both the academic and professional aspects of the field.
4. We caution against creation of public relations programmes at every university until such time as there are adequately qualified instructors. We would prefer to see one university develop a solid programme with five faculty members than to see five universities house programmes with one faculty member each.
5. There should be a standardised approach to programmes of education and professional advancement for those working in public relations. These educational opportunities should branch, out into related disciplines in addition to providing refresher courses in professional subjects.
6. IPRA should act as a clearing house between public relations bodies and university authorities.
7. Regional meetings should be arranged by IPRA in 1983 in order to assess the progress made since the publication of this Gold Paper at the, 9th Public Relations World Congress in Mumbai in January, 1982.
8. IPRA representatives and representatives of regional and national public relations associations should arrange discussions in and between their

organisations on how to make the best, use of this Gold Paper in their areas,

9. These associations should arrange conferences with university bodies in their areas to establish a better rapport between the professional field and the academia.
10. Report from such meetings should be forwarded to regional associations and to the IPRA. Education and Research Committee to keep these bodies updated on progress and to make them capable of acting as centres of information.
11. It is neither desirable nor necessary that public relations education should be uniform throughout the world. Rather it is essential that curricula should take into account local and national cultures, religions and indigenous conditions.
12. Positive efforts should be made to bring about a continuing dialogue between academics and professionals for their mutual benefit.
13. Research— both pure and applied— should be encouraged in educational spheres and in practice. Methods of evaluation of results should be investigated.
14. Professional advancement programmes should be expanded in all countries.
15. An increase in the quality and quantity of public relations textbooks and papers should be encouraged by all practical means.
16. There should be a regular interchange of information and ideas between public relations educators in different countries. This can be effected at congresses, through the public relations press and by direct contact.

17. Education and professional advancement programmes should be given priority by all national and regional public relations associations.
18. Introducing Public Relations Education where it is nonexistent at present: In countries where public relations education does not exist at university, level, at business schools or at other institutes of higher education, the following steps are recommended.
    - (i) The national public relations association in the country concerned should develop or initiate educational courses at appropriate levels.
    - (ii) The national association should establish a dialogue with universities with a view to the introduction of public relations education at undergraduate and graduate levels.
    - (iii) Approach should be made to business schools and management courses for the introduction into management studies of public relation's sequences, or at least an 'overview' course in the subject.
    - (iv) Steps should be taken to establish a library and resource centre for public relations and related material.
    - (v) Attention should be given to the possibility of tapping Governmental Aid Agencies and other potential sources of finance for implementing the previous suggestions.
    - (vi) Practitioners, educators and students should be encouraged to take advantage of short-term and longer term courses in other countries.

(vii) The advice of IPRA should be sought as appropriate so that all available sources of help and guidance be investigated and tapped.

Public Relations Education in India

In the Indian context some of the important features of Public Relations education can be summarises as follows:

(a) A major segement of Indian population (i.e. about 70%) is dependent on agriculture. And even agriculture is in the main carried on by primitive and age-old methods of cultivation resulting in a low level of productivity. However, there are a few pockets, where modern techniques of cultivation are followed and productivity is high.

(b) Organised industry in India currently absorbs hardly 2 to 3 per cent of the population. Small scale and cottage industry and retail trade absorb the rest of the urban population. Productivity in this unorganised sector is low.

(c) Population in India has been growing at a very high rate, about 2.5 per cent per annum in the last few decades.

(d) Living standards are low and more than 50 per cent of the population is living below the poverty line which in India means a per capita income level of less than 200 US$ per annum.

(e) About 70% of the population is illiterate. And of the remaining 30 per cent who are literate, the percentage of those who have been through Secondary schools would be hardly 10 per cent. Though in recent years same improvement is recorded in literacy ratio.

(f) India is a multilingual, multiracial and multicultural society. No doubt, politically a sense of nationhood has undoubtedly developed and economically the country comprises a single market, culturally instead, of a common composite culture emerging, there are at latest 15 or 16 distinct cultural groups with their own language, their own way of living. Linguistic and cultural differences are not disappearing but growing sharper.

(g) India is a land of contrasts. Side by side with primitive methods of agriculture, there are pockets where the yield of wheat for instance is as high as in the United States of America if not even higher. India has a highly developed Steel and Heavy Engineering industry, sophisticated petrochemical complexes and refineries, one of the largest railway systems in the world and is exporting turnkey projects and technological know-how in certain fields to countries abroad, including, some of the developed countries. India in fact, ranks 7th among the industrialised nations of the world. There is a developed infrastructure of technical training institutes, scientific establishments and laboratories. India has the third largest number of trained scinetific and technical manpower in the world. Of late India has made remarkable progress in the field of IT.

(h) Despite having a free market economy the public or government sector still controls all the strategic sectors of industry and that industry and commerce are subject to a plethora of controls and regulations and the complexities of the tasks confronting public relations practitioners in India become apparent.

Under such circumstances, public relations practitioners need to have certain qualities and personality traits without which it would not be possible for them to cope successfully with the problems constantly being, thrown up by the society around, them.

One of the most important requirements is that Public Relations men must have a scientific outlook and a modern mind. In the developing countries a constant, battle is raging between tradition and modernity. The process of industrialisation, the frequent contacts with the developed countries, the inflow of modern technology and the need for modernisation of agriculture itself to provide sustenance, to a burgeoning population all act as agents of change driving these countries in the direction of modernity. But the shackles binding them to the past are too powerful to be snapped easily.

Moreover, growing awareness of the effects, of excessive industrialisation such as environmental pollution, break up of family ties, emergence of new values tends to produce a backlash which often leads even highly educated intellectuals to question the need for industrialisation and modernisation. Evidently the developing countries cannot afford to follow mechanically the example of the advanced, industrial countries. Science and technology imported from the Western world must be judiciously blended with what is best, in the local culture and adapted to indigenous requirements. The public relations practitioner has an important role to play in influencing opinion leaders and decision-makers in their countries to take a balanced view for achieving emphatic results.

Whereas an ability to use the latest tools and techniques of public relations is essential, the skills required to operation as complicated an environment as exists in Indiahave to be a very high order indeed. Communication with vast masses of people who cannot read or write, who are still inaccessible in remote rural or hilly areas on the one hand and with the emerging elite on the other, makes it necessary or develop creative abilities. Communications even to the literate masses who are so diverse in background in culture cannot be carried on by routine methods in general. A constant process of experimentation, learning and research are called for.

Thus, it is evident that the task of preparing and educating public relations men and women in a country like India is not easy task. The first generation of public relations professionals in India acquired their skills on the job. Having come into the profession either via journalism or via advertising they learnt by trial and error, by experimentation and of course also from books on public relations published elsewhere. Using their own knowledge of the environment, they tried to adapt the principles and techniques of public relations as practised abroad to local conditions and requirements.

Now especially in the last few years, the position has changed a lot. A conscious attempt is being made to impart training to new entrants to the profession or to those aspiring to join its ranks. Simultaneously, senior practitioners are trying to improve their skills and to make themselves more effective by learning from one another's experience as also from available public relation literature from abroad or currently, being produced indigenously and trying to generalise and conceptualise on the experience gained by each one of them.

Classification

The types of educational activities that are going on in India may be categorised into the following groups:

1. Seminars, Workshops, Discussion Groups

Under the Public Relations Society of India (RSI), there are a number of Chapters and the Chapters generally hold one meeting every month and two to three seminars/ workshops a, year. At these meetings/seminars etc. sometimes experts from outside the profession are invited and on other occasions public relations practitioners themselves present papers and hold discussions on various problems being encountered .

2. Long-term Courses

Long-term courses are organised for public relations practitioners by the Chapters. In many cases, senior practitioners from the various Chapters of the PRSI provide the faculty while various colleges and institutes make all the organisational arrangements. In Mumbai, an eight-month diploma course is being organised by Bhavan's College and Xavier's College. The diploma course consists of seven lectures four days a week, special assignments once a week on subjects covered the syllabus, visits to establishments such as newspaper offices, printers, block makers, the television centres, public relations departments of various organisations, etc. Workshops on selected subjects where specialisation is needed are also organised as part of the course. A terminal examination is held midway during the course and a final examination at the end of the course. Successful students who wish to get an opportunity for practical training are assigned to public relations departments of large corporations for short periods.

Currently many colleges which are conducting courses on journalism or in advertising and marketing or in business management also cover public relations as part of the syllabus and here too public relations practitioners are invited to act as the faculty. This is the case, for instance, in the Department of Journalism, Calcutta University. Institute of Social Welfare and Business Management, affiliated to Calcutta University and the Indian Institute of Management, Kolkata.

3. *Short-term Training Courses*

Short-term training course for junior level public relations men are organised by the various Chapters of the PRSI from time to time. The faculty consists of senior public relations practitioners and people from different management disciplines as well as professors from academic institutions. Some of these short-term courses are held in collaboration with local management associations or other management institutes.

4. *Degree Courses*

The University of Madras, Chennai has a degree course, in public relations. A number of colleges affiliated to Madras University, such as the Government Art College, Stella Maris College, Nandanam College and Islamia College, run these courses. An average intake of about 20 students are enrolling in each of these colleges every year. A post-graduate diploma course in certain subjects related to public relations has also been started by the Madras University.

The Osmania University, Hyderabad is running a degree course as well Masters' course in Journalism and Communications. As part of the syllabus of courses they have papers on public relations and its various aspects.

5. *Institute of Mass Communications, Government of India*

Besides from this, there is an Institute of Mass Communication run by the Government of India. Courses on various aspects of mass communications are taught in which not only Indian students but also students from many Asian and African countries participate. Most of the courses are being run to prepare Information Officers for the Government of India and various Asian and African Governments. Under the auspices of the Institute of Mass Communications, public relations courses have also been organised for public relations practitioners in the public or Government sector.

Case Histories

Realising the importance of case histories in any educational programme and having regard to the fact that case histories based on a totally different environment would not be suitable for training programmes, in India, an effort is being made to prepare a number of case histories involving use of public relations techniques in different situations in special context of the country..

Syllabus

Based on the experience of the courses being conducted in various parts of India, the National Council of the Public Relations Society of India has prepared a standard syllabus for a short-term as well as an advanced long-term course. Most of the courses now being conducted are based on this syllabus that has been prepared by PRSI.

Barriers Encountered

A common complaint of public relations practitioners in India is that they are not being given the status that they deserve and public relations inputs are not being used in management decision-making. On behalf of management on the other hand, it is often stated that they are not getting the right type of public relations men and hence they do not feel they would benefit by taking their advice. Owing to the limited career opportunities in public relations and the failure on the part of top management in most organisations to give public relations the recognition it deserves the calibre of the people who are currently seeking admission into public relations is not always of a very high order. Management feels that the right type of public relations people are not available. And the right young people aspiring for a career in business and industry prefer other management disciplines such as finance of marketing or personnel rather than public relations. This vicious circle can only be broken by a concerted effort to educate people in public relations and to ensure that those thus trained are able to make a contribution to management decision-making.

A One more hurdle is that there is a serious lack of educators (i.e. trainers). Almost the entire burden of imparting education in public relations is being borne by the first generation of public relations practitioners who have been trained on the job and who while being well qualified from the point of view of their extensive experience have however limitations in certain spheres such as teaching technology and methods of carrying on research in public relations, etc.

Besides this, another problem is that so far the major institutes of management have failed to accept public relations as a management discipline in its own right Public relations is either ignored altogether or covered very inadequately as part of the marketing syllabus or so.

Ultimately, there is the need for carrying on original research on various issues of importance in so far as public relations in India is concerned.

The Indian Foundation for Public Relations Education and Research (IFPR) has been established by the Public Relations Society of India. IFPR as a registered non-profit organisation, established with a view to promote the role of Public Relations and Communications in modern business and more specifically for providing an academic and a professional base for education and training in Public Relations and allied disciplines of mass communication. The Foundation seeks to promote high professional standards in the practice of public relations and thus help facilitate the development, recognition and understanding of the role and value of Public Relations as a Management discipline. And shall be responsibility of the Foundation to provide and ensure a sound educational and intellectual base for the Public Relations practitioner through a system of examinations, certification and accreditation based on certain academic standards.

With a professional background in Public Relations, management recognition and appreciation will enhance; there will also be some uniformity in standards of training. Efforts will be made to obtain Government recognition for these Diplomas, Certification and Accreditation and employers will be urged to select Fellows, Associates or Diploma Holders of the Foundation, for filling up Public Relations vacancies at all levels both in public sector and private sector, as well as Government agencies and other institutions.

Over a period of time professionals from such diversified backgrounds, when continue to perform same or similar functions, certain common problems and consensus to overcome problems are bound to emerge among them. In such situations they are also bound to take certain actions to avoid such problems in future. This in turn helps them to evolve professional ethics and philosophy and establish related parameters in terms of educational qualifications, the quality and quantity of experience they would like professionals to get exposed during their working, their professional activities and the degree of interaction among them on professional issues.

Educational Qualifications

Although it is a fact that majority of the existing practitioners in the profession did not have any formal qualifications in Public Relations, but the advantages of professional qualifications can hardly be denied. Some of the existing practitioners who are commercially and professionally very well accepted, may discount the role of professional qualifications in Public Relations by citing their own example, yet they cannot imagine how well they would have done had they acquired the same. But if they advocate the same approach and wish their successors to come through hit and trial method, then that reflects a narrowness of attitude towards their profession and its growth. This approach would be no different from the approach of their predecessors from whom they learned work. Their best contribution, therefore, will be to make things simpler, easy and acceptable for the new entrants to the profession by ensuring that their experiences are passed on to the next generation along with their suggestions for improvement.

Enforcing professional qualifications for the new entrants will thus be a step in the right direction. Most of the existing practitioners have acquired educational qualifications upto graduation level, while the second category of practitioners have done some part time diploma in public relations or journalism, graphics, marketing or advertising etc. The third category of the practitioners have acquired Masters of Business Administration with specialisation in marketing either from Indian universities or institutes or foreign universities/institutes. A negligible percentage of existing practitioners have acquired specialised qualifications in Public Relations from foreign universities/ institutes or Indian institutes. It is this heterogeneity of educational background of the existing practitioners which is responsible for the diversity in their values, philosophy and attitude towards their profession.

If the profession has to achieve its rightful status in the society, it is high time that the existing practitioners collectively apply themselves to introduce specialised courses in Public Relations through well designed curriculum by impressing upon institutions like University Grants Commission and other private institutions. It is worthwhile to keep in mind the following recommendations of the Education and Research Committee of the International Public Relations Association issued in January 1982 while designing Public Relations courses in India:

(a) Two years full time or part time Master's degree should be introduced by Universities and various educational institutes in Public Relations including subjects like journalism, advertising, personnel management, marketing management, and graphics, layout and design, social research & statistics etc. Public Relations full time education should be offered in Universities at the Master's degree level.

(b) Public Relations should by preference be taught as a social science with both academic and professional emphasis.

(c) It is neither desirable nor necessary that Public Relations education should be uniform throughout the world. Rather it is essential that curriculum should take into account local and national cultures, religions and indigenous conditions.

Depending upon the recommendations of professional bodies like Public Relations Society of India and its acceptance and implementation by various educational Institutes, their programmes and courses should be accredited by it. Students passing out from such accredited Institutes should be recommended by Public Relations Society of India to its member companies for appointment as public relations practitioners.

11

Management-Employee Relations

From the Public Relations point of view change in the quality of workers in India during the past few decades, especially in the period after independence is of prime importance. Industrial development prior to independence was not encouraged by the then government of the country. The railways and ancillary industries to meet the needs of the railways came up, coal mining, jute and cotton textile industries came up in the middle of nineteenth century. Tea plantations were started at about the same time. Indian labour did not originate as in some of the Western countries from the artisans in the towns. It consisted mostly of migrants from the villages usually from the lower castes. Workers were mostly illiterate and had little awareness of their rights. Not that many rights existed in the early period. The Trade Union Act giving the right to workers to organise themselves came as late as 1926. The Payment of Wages Act was passed in 1936 and the Factories Act in 1948. The first attempts to improve the conditions of the workers were made by social reformers, at a later stage the leaders of the national movement realising the importance of mobilising a vast and strategically important sector of the population in support of the freedom struggle also played attractive role in organising workers movements.

Gradually, the situation has been changing after Independence. Fairly powerful trade union organisations have sprang up and a considerable amount of legislation protecting the rights of the workers, regulating wages, hours of work, conditions of work especially in respect of safety has been passed, by the Parliament and the State legislatures. But the legacy of the past has not been obliterated completely. The links with the land and the rural orientation is still to be found among a large number of workers.

As yet outsiders play an important, in some cases a dominant role. The multiplicity of trade unions and their fragmentation is another offshoot of the same phenomenon. Trade Unions are mostly under the influence of political parties and as political parties have multiplied and fragmented so have the trade unions led by them. Multiple trade unions in the same industry or unit leads often to bitter inter-union rivalry which is an obstacle to healthy collective bargaining between management and labour which is a basic feature of an industrial society.

It must be remembered that the first industries in India were started either by traders and elements of the landed gentry who invested their surplus in industrial units or by the British managing agencies who brought expatriates from abroad to run these industries. Today industries in the private sector can broadly be classified in to two industries. There are the family owned and largely family managed industries and there are the professionally managed companies many of which are associated with large transnational corporations. However this description needs to be qualified in so far as even family owned businesses are now inducting a large number of professional managers into their organisations. Moreover the younger generation of business owning families is now undergoing training in various management institutes or IITs and some are even going abroad for education.

Notably at every stage of operation management and

employees have to interact. Whether it is the purchase and storing of raw materials and spares, whether it is production,, distribution or marketing, harmonious relations between management and labour are the essential prerequisites for a healthy bottom line. Since the management of employees is a very complex matter involving or compliance of a number statutory provisions, negotiations with trade unions an a working out of agreements, the hammering out of wage policies, the development of skills, working out of productivity norms and numerous other aspects of the development and deployment of the human resources of an organisations. Despite the existence of many special departments, it may be termed the Public Relations Department also has to play a role in this area of the company's management as in many other areas such as marketing, finance, secretarial and so on.

Labour legislation has come into being in big way in India where the government is committed to the principles of a welfare state and to the building up of a socialistic pattern of society. For example, there is the Payment of Wages Act, the Factories Act, the Contract Labour (Regulation and Abolition) Act, Equal Remuneration Act, the Payment of Bonus Act, the Industrial Disputes Act, the Industrial Employment (Standing Orders) Act besides various laws providing for safety measures, proper environment and other amenities. Besides, there are various decisions of tripartite bodies which even though not embodied in the form of an act are for all practical purposes binding on employers and employees alike such as the Code of Discipline. One of the important functions of the Personnel. Department of an organisation is to ensure that the organisation complies with these laws and decisions. Another important area of functioning for this department is to carry on bargaining with the workers' representatives though in important matters the top management of an organisation has to take the decisions.

As such a major part of management the public relations department is not directly involved in industrial relations. As is inevitable disputes between management and labour arise from time to time and this sometimes leads to a situation of conflict or confrontation. In this confrontation it is the Personnel Department that represents one side, the management side while the trade unions represent the other side. The Public Relations Department by not being directly involved in such situations is in a relatively advantageous situation as its role is not perceived by employees as that of an adversary. The Public Relations Department must therefore try to earn the trust of employees as a credible source of information. The task of giving workers a sense of belonging to the organisation, of developing positive attitude towards the company in which they are working rests largely on the Public Relations Department. This can best be achieved by keeping workers informed of the developments within the company, taking them into confidence with regard to the problems and difficulties the organisation is facing and thus treating them as mature partners in the enterprise rather than as mere cogs in a vast impersonal machine.

As a general practice, 'communication' is often carried out in a casual manner, more as a ritual than as a meaningful tool in a total exercise to develop harmonious employer-employee relations. The House Journal can prove to be the most important vehicle of internal communication but more often than not it is treated as a status symbol. The quality of pictures, printing, design and layout are given the main importance not the quality of the contents, its newsworthiness and its role as a purveyor of information.

An obsession with the form and the design results in inordinate delays and even important pieces of news lose all their significance by being dished out long after the event. It must be remembered that the House Journal is a channel of three way communication. It conveys news of what the organisation is doing, where it is going, what it is planing to do and what these plans mean for the employees in terms of their prospects, opportunities of promotion and advancement and so on. It also conveys news of what employees are doing, what they are achieving and what problems they are facing. The House Journal should also reflect management thinking and their views on various matters of interest to the organisation and to the employees. At the same time the House Journal should provided a forum for the employees to express their views, to give their suggestions, raise problems, ask questions, even to criticise when they feel it necessary to do so. The management can always append its own point of view side by side. It is only by doing this that the journal will achieve credibility. The need to communicate in time can not be overemphsised. If an organisation is bent on producing a glossy pictorial magazine media must be devised for more frequent and faster dissemination of information.

The development of new technologies such as laser printing, computer printing, etc., provide opportunity to print newssheets fast and to distribute them rapidly throughout the organisation. Advantage can be taken of this but where necessary even the older technology of cyclostyling can be effectively used. Regular and frequent communication, once a week or so and not once in three months or six months is what is required. Other media of internal communication should not be ignored. The notice board, the poster, personal contact, group meetings and various types of audio-visual communication can and should be used depending on the need and the situation. As will be seen when we go into actual case histories and examples, today companies are taking full advantage of developments in technology and internal public address systems, cable television and videos are being used.

The task of communicating to the mass of employees is left exclusively to the unions in some organisations. Union leaderships in some cases go to the extent of resenting direct communication by the employers to workers and even make this the subject of an industrial dispute. This happens particularly when management and employees are on a confrontational course. This is clearly not a very desirable situation even from the standpoint of the employees. Employees should be exposed to all points of view and if the union case is strong, the union leadership should have the confidence of being able to carry the workers with them despite the management viewpoint being communicated to them. This is the essence of democratic functioning and this also protects workers from being misled by a coterie of unscrupulous leaders who might be trying to make them act in their own interests rather than in the interests of the employees as a wholes. In organisations where communication by the management is a normal practice and is carried on as a regular exercise the problem is not likely to arise.

This leads on to the question of communicating in a strike situation. A lockout or other forms of crisis would also need similar treatment. In situations of this kind passions tend to be roused and an atmosphere of tension and bitterness prevails. The first thing to remember in such a situation is that the effort should be to look beyond the immediate and to avoid saying or doing anything that would accentuate the bitterness, lead to further excitement and reduce the chances of a settlement. Ultimately management and labour would have to work together again if the organisation is to survive and the effort should therefore be to adopt a conciliatory tone, to convey the correct information and not to distort facts or to exaggerate things. In particular all communications from the Public Relations Department should be factual and couched in sober language.

While the Personnel Department or other authorised representatives of the top management will maintain formal contact with the Labour Department, Home Department and other concerned ministries the PR department should send copies of press releases, other informative material, with regard to the issues involved in an easily readable form and presented as briefly as possible. It is desirable in normal cases to keep the dialogue with the union going. This will be conducted at the formal level by the personnel department but the PR department can carry on the dialogue through informal channels taking care to see however that the two departments do not work at cross purposes and the efforts of the two are coordinated with the approval of top management. Some companies put out paid advertisements in the press giving their point of view and their version of the facts. As far as possible this should be avoided. If the company has a good case it should be possible to get the press to report it in its news and editorial columns.

Paid advertising tends to create greater bitterness amongst employees as they have a feeling that money power is being used to give the company an unfair advantage. Moreover it tends to antagonise the general public too which tends to side with the underdog.

12

Public Relations with External Publics

The various constituents of external publics are Customers, community, mass media, Government, financial institutions, action groups and general public are the various constituents of external publics.

1. *Consuiners (or Customers):* The management era of modern times belongs to marketing where every thing happening in the company revolves around the customer. In the words of Mahatma Gandhi, "a customer is not a means of business, but he is the purpose of business. He is not a intruder on our premises, he is our guest. He is the last inspector of our quality and he is always right". These few lines by him very aptly describe the philosophy of marketing and the importance of the customer. The concept of modern enterprise starts with customer, keeping in mind his needs, choice, preferences, taste, paying capacity etc., and ends up with satisfying his needs to *his* utmost satisfaction. It includes existing customers as well as probable customers and future customers. A person who may belong to the category of general public today, may become the customer of the company's products or services in future depending upon his opinion and the goodwill of the company.

2. *Mass Media:* Press is one of the major sources of mass media. With the improvement in transportation system and increase in the literacy rate, newspapers, magazines,

story books, comics, weekly newspapers etc., are becoming more popular in rural and semi-urban areas also. Similarly the coverage of 88 per cent of the total population of the country through television network has been a major achievement of post-Independence era. Both the developments have significantly added to the value of mass media and its importance in improving and establishing favourable public relations. Many Public Relations professionals believe that with the increasing popularity of electronic media, print media will lose its importance. The figures published by Registrar of Newspapers of India, Audit Bureau of Circulation for publications on national as well as regional level show a constant increase in the circulation of various newspapers, magazines and periodicals disproves this perception. Mass media have always remained a very strong source of voicing opinion, building propaganda and influencing the behaviour of the masses and it will remain so in the future as well.

3. *Community:* Community as a whole represents that public which stays in the close vicinity of the organisation, its office, plants and godown, warehouse etc. These people undergo change in their lifestyle depending upon the business activities of the organisation. The increasing cost of living, congestion, pollution, health hazards, sanitation and various social problems like drinking, gambling, prostitution etc., near various large companies in India are testimony of the transformation a company brings in its neighbourhood. Therefore, it becomes a social and moral obligation of the industry to compensate community for these losses by making its humble contribution to improve their living in some way. It includes providing employment to the community members as far as possible, providing health services in the form of dispensary, hospital

and nursing homes, education and environment protection etc.

4. Government: Where mixed economy is the declared policy of the Government, like India all the major institutions for control of trade, business and industry are with the Government right from licensing, regulatory powers, distribution network, import-export of raw materials, finished product, technology and machinery imports and even price control power for certain industries, all are vested in Government. Taxation and revenue policy itself is the most effective weapon in the hands of Government. The Government exercises its control over trade, commerce and industry at three levels i.e. district level, state level and Central or national level. There are inconsistencies in the policies of state and central governments, particularly if they are ruled by two different political parties. Even at the implementation level, there are differences of opinion in the hierarchy of implementation machinery. The full impact of new policy of liberalisation is yet to unfold itself fully and may take time to trickle to the grassroot level. On a single subject like labour, there are at present more than 140 legislations, virtually making it impossible even for a most honest company to ensure compliance. The procedures are complicated and cumbersome. In such a environment, the dependence of industry, trade and commerce on Government is all the more obvious. From the point of view of public relations, Government and its machinery can be divided in to two distinct categories depending on their characteristics i.e. politicians and bureaucrats. The public relations professionals have to ensure that without hurting the feelings of either of them and equally balancing their relationship with them, they have to pursue the objectives of their company, department and the profession.

5. Action Groups: The concept of an Action Group is relatively new in India and within a short span, it has become very popular. The enactment of Consumer Protection Act, 1986, has been a major milestone in this regard. Although the rules were framed in 1987 under the Consumer Protection Act, but both central as well as state governments did not take any action for providing appropriate machinery under the Act and the rules till one advocate filed a special writ petition in Supreme Court in 1990 for issuance of directives to States as well as Central Government to provide appropriate machinery. Prior to Consumer Protection Act, the lawyers, solicitors, jurists, press, bureaucrats and various religious groups used to act as action groups depending upon the subject matter, controversy or the dispute between the company and these groups.

6. Financial Institutions: The relationship with financial institutions has always been very important for business. Whether it is the normal banking facilities like overdraft or credit or merchant banking, companies heavily are dependent on the functioning and the patronage of financial institutions at the branch, zonal headquarters levels. The financial institutions have very important role in all commercial transactions of the company, commencement of business, its expansion and growth and even its retardation. Before the commencement and financing of the project, it is the financial institutions who undertake project appraisal, whether it is a viable project or not and thereafter for extending banking and credit facilities, additional funds for growth and expansion and providing additional working capital in case of cost overruns or delay in implementation of project. The financial institutions in our country can be divided into three categories i.e. public sector banks, private sector banks and foreign banks.

The majority of the business is with the public sector banks due to over protective policies of the Government. Now the situation changed drastically.

7. *General Public:* They are the largest of all the external publics of an organisation and probably the most tolerant of all the publics who watch the various practices, good or bad, of the company without reacting much. Yet, they are the one who matter most in the ultimate analysis of the functioning of the company. They are the most misunderstood public as every one takes them for granted, but they have a definite outlook and definite opinion which emerges over a period of time. Unlike other publics where one could get to see its response or reaction instantly, here due to large size and huge geographical spread-out it takes a much longer time to get the response, it has its own values, culture, language, views and relationship with different companies depending on how they respond to their needs and what its outlook is towards them.

Significance of External Publics

The significance of external publics can be made out from this fact that without them, a company cannot exist. These include the customers, community, mass media, Government, financial institutions, action groups and general public. Undoubtedly, most of the companies in our country as of now take a very casual and problem/ project based approach towards them, but very soon they will be compelled by circumstances of increasing competition, government regulatory and taxation policy, role of financial institutions and active role and close scrutiny by various action groups and general public to mend their ways. Obviously this is going to be very painful for such companies to accept and adopt themselves to the changed environment. Even according to theory 'Z' of motivation, the employees of a company can be motivated after a certain extent by showing their contribution to the society alone.

Relations with External Publics

The success of any enterprise of any organisation depends on how well it adopts and relates with its external publics. It should not only be fair in its approach to them but should also appear to be fair. The rapport building and establishing meaningful channels of communication with each of these publics is the art and science of public relations. The concept is changing from public relations in marketing to marketing of public relations services and activities.

Customer Relations: Customer is the centre of today's business activities. Apart from providing a quality product at a reasonable price at customer's doorsteps, a company has to constantly keep in touch with its customers to find out their responses towards various changes incorporated by the company in its functioning. Market research, public opinion polls, customer satisfaction level and after-sales services have never engaged so much attention of the companies as it is doing today. Customer education, customer opinion and customer services have become the main business concern of company.

Community Relations: The community has to undergo a lot of social, political, cultural and economic changes because of the business activity of the an organisation. As a gratitude and compensation towards this contribution of community, companies provide various types of health services, education service, sewage and sanitation facilities etc. Giving preference to community people in employment, making suppliers and developing dealers, distributors and retailers out of them apart from serving companies business interest strengthen the relations with community. Participation in community's social and cultural functions, making generous contribution towards its success by giving donation and infrastructural support leads to good will and longer lasting relations.

Media Relations: In a competitive world where too many companies are trying to develop relations with media with various types of attractions offered to them, how does one get an edge over his competitors? The only answer to this question is competence, decency and a caring attitude. The wining, dining, gifting or palm-greasing image of pubic relations practitioners is greatly due to how they interact with media. If is a relationship which has to be nurtured over a period of time and shortcuts through wining and dining approach will be suicidal from long-term prospective. After providing the intellectual food to the media, normal courtesy and caring attitude will strengthen the relationship whereas too much emphasis on eating, drinking, gifts etc., without appropriate briefing will on the contrary expose the hollowness of Public Relations practitioners and his company.

Government Relations: Various expressions like lobbying, liaison, Public Relations etc., with Government today are most misunderstood. Because of the manner it has been handled by the existing practitioners of public relations leading to scandals and scams in our country that no Government official worth his salt will associate himself with them. The real purpose of this relationship seems to be disappearing because of vested interests of individual practitioners, their company and in some case the industry as a whole. The Public Relations professionals have to prevail upon their companies and industry as a whole to reverse such unhealthy and undesirable practices.

Relations with Financial Institutions: The relationship with financial institutions has to be built on the basis of willing cooperation by the company in furnishing the information sought by them. The company must adopt a policy, of open and frank dialogue with them regarding their problems and seek their expertise in resolving the same. The presentation of their case through arranging a visit to site and plant, giving details of their projects, technical know-how, technical and financial collaboration and market projection helps the financial institutions to understand the company's plans better as a result of which they are able to contribute their best and gain the confidence about the company. Timely submission of progress reports, payment of principal and interest amount and keeping them abreast with the latest relevant information further helps the company to strengthen its credibility and goodwill with the financial institution.

Relations with General Public: General public is the ultimate judge of all the activities of the company, based on which it will survive or die. Interaction with general public is through mass media like newspapers, magazines, Radio, Television, exhibitions, banners, hoardings, leaflets etc. One of major sources of sustaining and developing relations with general public is through advertising. More and more companies are realising the importance of public relations advertising where instead of concentrating on the 'Product' or the 'Brand' image-building, companies are showing an increased concern for various social issues such as illiteracy, environment protection, pollution control to improve the quality of life of public to create more responsible images of their companies. This shift from institutional advertising to image advertising is to show the concern of the company for public interest. It is a vital shift from what the company is done why it is doing these good things for public.

Relations with Action Groups: Although less in numbers, but very high in terms of their potential to harm or influence the interests of the company are the Action Groups. Relationship with them is to be developed to find out their attitude and the line of action with the company. The peculiarity of this group is that they expect an immediate response to their communications and a regular contact with the company. They have a high ego and esteem profile because of their position of power, credibility and ability to influence masses. In order to initiate healthy relationship with them, public relations professionals should initiate regular dialogue with them once in a while over a social issue in an informal exclusive gathering. They should also be included in the Public Relations list of the company so that they get Public Relations literature of the company regularly and are invited to all the social and cultural functions of the company to create a positive image of company in their mind.

External Communications

The quality of competence, work and performance of Public Relations professionals is judged or ascertained on the basis of various communications designed by them for communicating with various publics. While in internal communication the emphasis is on developing specific message for each group of internal publics to make it more target-oriented, the emphasis in external communication is to make it more general so that it can make sense to people from different backgrounds, caste, creed, sex, age etc. The coverage and cost of the message are directly proportionate to each other and in order to create the desired impact, the frequency of repetition of message has to be predetermined. Keeping in view the vastness of the public, their location, their lifestyle, preference, taste and the time at their disposal, the company has to make use of a variety of media to reach them. Wall paintings, dance dramas, exhibitions, video and feature films are very effective methods of communicating with rural population while in semi-urban, urban and metropolitan cities advertisements in newspapers, magazines, periodicals, television and video films have proved more effective. Sponsoring social and entertainment programmes on television, satellite television and video channels is becoming very popular with masses as a media of communication and has already become part of public relations advertising.

The quality of message is becoming more important than the frequency of repetition as people and other publics are becoming more quality conscious. The emphasis of the message is shifting from need-orientation to interest-orientation. Companies will serve the educational and social interests of the publics more than anything else. The publics are also getting conscious of the facts that cost of advertising and other media are passed on to them by companies in the form of increased prices of their products or services. Therefore, instead of blindly increasing the advertising and publicity budget of the companies, it will be better to say *less but more effectively* rather than irritating publics with repeated advertisement exposure.

Summing Up

It is the image and credibility it enjoys in the minds of external publics which makes an organisation successful. It may have many internal problems but if it is enjoying good image and credibility in the market, it will always get support from the external publics to tide over its internal problems. However, it is not to suggest that a company could ignore its internal publics because it can get the help and cooperation of the external publics as and when it is needed. On the contrary, it is absolutely essential that a company should have very good relationship with its internal publics in order to gain the confidence and cooperation of its external publics.

REFERENCES

1. Kolter, Philip, *Marketing Management Analysis, Planning and Control,* Prentice Hall of India (Pvt.) Ltd., New Delhi.
2. Mehta, D.S. (1992), "A Public Relations fob" *Hindustan Times,* Sunday-Supplement dated 11th October.
3. Rotman, Morris B. (1974), *'PR is Still Necessary Adjunct to Efficient Marketing Today'* Advertising & Sales Promotion.
4. Seitel, Fraser P. & Charles E., *The Practice of Public Relations,* Merrill Publishing Co. A Bell & Howell Company, Columbus.

13

Career in Public Relations

The fact that, unlike most other professions, lack of a qualifying degree or diploma in Public Relations is as yet no bar to entry into the profession, makes it relatively easy to sneak in and also makes the profession a happy hunting ground for adventurers of various hues. But the days of such adventurers are now numbered. The way is being cleared for the genuine professionals who already outnumber those who have just drifted in.

Public Relations is now a vocation and persons who wish to take it up should begin by asking themselves if they are suited to it. If not, they should choose a calling that is more in line with, their temperament and abilities.

Prerequisites of Public Relations Man

Edward L. Bernays, one of the founders of Public Relations in the United States says, "I think that the ideal public relations man should first of all, be a man of character and integrity, who has acquired a sense of judgement and logic without having lost the ability to think creatively and imaginatively. He should be truthful and discreet; he should be objective, yet possessed of a deep interest in the solution of problems. From his broad cultural background, he should I have developed considerable intellectual curiosity; and he should have effective powers of analysis and synthesis along with the rare quality of intuition. And with all these characteristics, he should be trained in the social sciences and in the mechanics of public relations."

1. *Character & Integrity:* Character and integrity are amongst the key attributes because this is a profession in which the Public Relations man will be exposed to the temptation of seeking shortcuts, of achieving his ends by any means. In taking an easy way out of a difficult situation he will be running the risk of ruining his own and his company's reputation. Character and integrity are necessary because the Public Relations man is the voice of conscience within the organisation. It is he who has to make it a good corporate citizen and if he himself lacks character how can he hope to build the image of his company?

Character and integrity are needed all the more because business is already held in suspicion by the general public as well as by the government.

2. *Courage:* The Public Relations man should possess courage. He should have courage to speak up when he feels that his organisation is taking a wrong course. He should have the courage to say no when the client he serves whether that be someone within his own organisation, or a client outside, asks him to do something which will not be in the public interest. He should have the courage of his conviction and not allow himself to be pressurised or influenced into doing something that is unethical. His function is to counsel and advise. It is naturally the prerogative of top management to decide. Even where, in the rare instance he happens to be part of top management his views in the top policy-making body may be overridden by the majority. What is his duty in such a situation? If he feels that the decision being taken or the course being followed is mistaken but the intentions behind it are honest, he should go along with the decision. The test of practice

will reveal whether his own judgement was wrong or whether it was the majority decision that was incorrect. In the latter case the top management will no doubt realise their error and their respect for the Public Relations man will grow.

On the other hand if he is proved wrong he should acknowledge his mistake with good, grace, and draw the right lesson for the future. If on the other hand the Public Relations man feels that the course of action is unethical and likely to harm public interest he must fight against it and if he fails to carry the majority with him should be prepared to submit his resignation. This undoubtedly requires courage of a high order but that is precisely what is expected of a Public Relations man. Some people wish to enter the profession of public relations just because they like to mix with people and think that this profession provides a good opportunity for meeting interesting people. True, the ability to mix with people, to create a good impression, is an asset for the Public Relations man. True also that the profession provides an opportunity to meet lots of interesting people. But the ability to mix with people is not the main quality required of a Public Relations man. A Public Relations man should not of course under any circumstances antagonise, people but even a quiet shy individual who does not mix well can be a successful Public Relations man if he has the ability to understand people, if he is a good judge of human character and if he can plan a communication campaign directed toward a group or groups of people effectively and intelligently.

In fact it is not the man with the big mouth the babbler, who is a good Public Relations man but the man who has a sense of discretion who can keep his counsel, whom the client whether his own top management or an outside party can trust and rely upon to keep a secret, who is best suited for the profession.

3. *Intellectual Attainment:* To be able to interpret the environment, to be able to understand different attitudes and appreciate shifts and changes that constantly take place in these attitudes, to be able to work out methods of influencing people individually and in groups, requires an understanding of economics, sociology and psychology. That is why it has been said that the Public Relations man must be something of a social scientist.

Particularly, Public Relations requires a thorough understanding of the social environment and an awareness of the process, of change that is constantly taking place within that environment. The physical environment changes slowly. For perceptible differences to manifest themselves in relation to the physical environment takes decades, even centuries. But the social and political environment changes rapidly from year to year, even month to month. Only a very alert mind which knows what changes it should be on the lookout for, which anticipates the, trends that are likely to emerge, can keep pace with the speed at which human society tends to move.

Incase of India, those who enter the field of Public Relations will be faced with a special problem which perhaps their counterparts in the advanced industrial countries do not have to contend with. Although the country has by now acquired a strong industrial infrastructure and has attained a fairly high level of technological advancement the superstructure in India has tended, to lag behind. Modern machinery and modern equipment is still largely handled by technicians and workers who retain traditional attitudes and even industrial management is still by and large run on traditional rather than on modern, scientific lines.

This poses two types of problems for Public Relations functionaries. The task of selling Public Relations in the full sense of the term to a management that is still largely moulded in the traditional pattern is by no means easy.

Even where a Public Relations department is maintained it is not effective if put to use for functions which do not really belong to it. The task of getting such a management to appreciate the true significance of Public Relations is an uphill one and often a frustrating experience. Secondly, it involves a very thorough understanding of the whole political and economic environment of the country. Without such an understanding no effective communication can take place with the Indian publics who are products of the very special kind of environment that exists in India. Above all it requires an ability to sympathise with the problems and difficulties that the masses in India are facing.

So much for the theoretical equipment and the attitudes needed in Public Relations but that only makes up one part of the requirement. Public Relations is not only a science but also an art and the Public Relations man should therefore be skilled in the art of communication, in the use of the multifarious media that modern technology has made available. Public Relations demands a special kind of outlook, a sense of vision, a fertile imagination a creative ability—in short intangible qualities that are difficult to define or catalogue but which are immediately recognisable when they are present in an individual.

To fulfil the task expected of him, a Public Relations man must make an attempt to understand the organisation in which he works, the principles and the philosophy that guide it, the problems that face it and the people who provide the leadership and make the decisions in the organisation. Management expects that public relations men will not only bring to the organisation their skills of communication their knowledge of the tools and the techniques bat they should also be able to tell the Management what is to be communicated and to do so they must begin with a very thorough study of the business or the businessness that are carried on by the organisation which they have come to serve. It is only by doing so that they will be able to draw up meaningful programmes and to help the organisation in working out the right equation with its publics. This is by no means an easy task because it requires some knowledge and some understanding of almost everyone of the various functions of a business organisation. A Public Relations man will not be able to suggest a strategy for shareholder communication, for example, if he does not have at least some idea of the financial structure of the organisation, of how it operates and what its plans are.

Similarly, if the Public Relations man does not have some understanding of the personnel policies pursued by the organisation he will not be able to assist in the vital tasks of internal communication which should be one of the major preoccupations of a Public Relations department Again, a knowledge of the products and the markets in which they are sold are necessary if the Public Relations department is to be in a position to help and advise the marketing managers of the organisation. Obviously the Public Relations man cannot be a specialist in every field but he should have sufficient understanding of the various functions and disciplines of the Management to be able to give advice to them on the Public Relations aspects of their work. The second requirement of a Public Relations department is an understanding of the nature of the political, economic and social environment of the country and of the region where the organisation to which it belongs is functioning. A specialist, no matter how qualified, will be ineffective if he does not have some knowledge of the nature of the publics in that particular country or region. The functioning of the Government and Parliament in India are quite different from the those say in Europe or Britain. Thus a Public Relations department to be effective needs to familiarise itself with the peculiarities and the idiosyncrasies of the people and the various segments of the public. Here again, public relations as a discipline is very different from certain other disciplines such as Finance or Engineering. While there are probably certain general principles of public relations that are valid for all situation and all environments, the importance of the specific situation and the specific environment is far greater in public relations than in other fields.

This is because, as the name itself suggests, public relations involves dealing with human beings and no two human beings are the same not to speak of groups and communities of men which differ from country to country and region to region. Having made this clear and dispelled any illusion that the task of public relations is merely a question of having certain, skills and a familiarity with certain tools and media of communication, it is necessary to point out that it is of course extremely important for a public relations department to have the requisite skills for putting across a message effectively and a thorough knowledge of the tools and media of communication.

This is specially so in the modern world where the number of people to whom the message is to be conveyed is growing larger and where the public may be spread across vast distances, sometimes scattered across the various continents of the world. Moreover, the tools and media of communications are also gradually growing more sophisticated and a Public Relations department which does not keep abreast of the latest technology in these fields will not be able to advise its Management about the bets way of sending out the message that needs to be conveyed.

Printing techniques have travelled a long way from the days when Johann Gutenberg set up his printing press at Germany in the 1450's. What techniques would be most suited for a particular type of publication, and for the particular public for whom it is meant is something that can only be decided if the costs and benefits of different techniques of printing are known. The same applies to the other media such as slides, films, posters. The Public Relations man should have sufficient knowledge of everyone of them to be able to advise Management on the suitability of a particular medium for a particular occasion. Coming to the question of the mode of functioning of a Public Relations department in a particular organisation it has to be appreciated that the Public Relations department has to function as a kind of service unit within the organisation. In relation to corporate matters, the Public Relations department must advise top Management on corporate policies that need to be adopted and in consultation with top Management will draw up and execute programmes to communicate the corporate message.

In most organisations, however, its responsibility will not end with that. The Public Relations department must also lend its services to the different divisions and departments of the organisation. It must assist divisional or departmental Management in drawing up communication programmes to suit their requirements and once these programmes have been agreed upon with the divisional departmental Management it must execute these programmes as effectively as possible.

As a consequence Public Relations in India is not yet universally accepted as one of the essential management functions. Even many of the large enterprises who would not dream of functioning without a team of accountants and auditors are blissfully unaware of the need for an organisation to maintain its accounts with the public, to have a, system of social audit.

But while an organisation may conceivably continue to function without full-fledge accounting section, it will be unable to survive for long if it suffers loss of public goodwill. Whether conscious of it or not Public Relations is to an extent practised by most organisations but in an amateurish way where it does not have a team of trained professionals to handle it. Gradually, however, the awareness of the need for Public Relations is growing. More and more organisations are setting up Public Relations departments or making use of Public Relations agents consultants. This is true of both the public and private sectors in India. It is particularly heartening to note that in the public sector a Public Relations set-up has now become an essential component of the organisation structure. In the private sector where Public Relations was first introduced it is unfortunately not as widespread as it should be.

In the modern age, ample opportunities are there of employment in Public Relations. Almost all Govt. departments, educational institutions, hospitals, industries and business houses have great scope of Public Relations men.

14

Financial Public Relations

After liberalisation of economy and globalisation era set in the phenomenal growth of the capital market in India has brought financial public relations to the centre of the PR stage. A very considerable part of the PR and advertising budget of companies is going into campaigns to promote new share issues, debentures, bonds and fixed deposits. Till some years ago loans from banks and certain long-term lending institutions were the main sources of finance for companies. However, the situation has now changed completely with the government having clearly indicated that companies should not rely on financial institutions but should more and more turn to the capital market for funds. The tremendous boom that has been witnessed is indicated by the fact that whereas a sometime ago average raisings from the capital market were about Rs. 100 crores they are now nearing a mark of around Rs. 10,000 crores per annum. However, even today financial institutions continue form an important source of funds and exert a tremendous, influence capital market as they operate on a large scale in the buying and selling of shares and other securities.

Mainly four categories of financing institutions are found in India including (a) The Central Government sponsored financial institutions namely, Industrial Development Bank of India (IDBI), Industrial Credit & Investment Corporation of India (ICICI), Industrial Finance

Corporation of India (IFCI) and Industrial Reconstruction Bank of India (IRBI), (b) Investment institutions namely, The Life Insurance Corporation of India (LICI), The Unit Trust of India (UTI) and the commercial banks, (c) The state level promotional agencies namely, the state industrial development corporations, and (d) The state level financial and small-scale industries development corporations.

Most relevantly, it is necessary to point out also that commercial loans from abroad are other sources of funds. These funds are either raised from the foreign money market and syndicated by foreign banks or by a consortium of Indian and foreign banks or are being directly raised from Non-Resident Indians (NRIs).

Besides these institutional investors, the emergence of a class of small investors from the middle classes and even from the other sections of the populations has added a new dimension to the capital market. The total population of shareholders which was less than 20 lakhs a few years ago has risen to over millions today. The increasing competition among companies to tap this market and its growing size, has made financial public relations such an important part of PR today. The objective of financial PR is first to build the companies' corporate image and particularly of their financial strength and viability and second to launch specific campaigns for promoting public issues, offers for sale, rights issues and fixed deposit schemes.

The target audience comprises the existing shareholders of the company, investors who normally invest funds and also a large section of the public who have savings but who may not be normally investing in equity issues, bonds, etc. The procedure usually adopted is to begin well before the time of the planned issue to build up the corporate image. This can take various forms such as: (i) meetings with financial correspondents; (ii) presentation of audio-visuals; (iii) meeting stock brokers; (iv) mailing of corporate brochures; and (v) institutional advertising campaign in the press and other media highlighting the financial strength of the organisation.

The next stage is the actual campaign to sell the issue. Again for this the steps taken are: (i) Pre-issue advertisements in newspapers and other media; (ii) Prospectus announcement; (iii) Press conferences; (iv) Brokers conferences; (v) Investors meetings; (vi) Mailing of brochures; and (viii) Posters, hoardings; etc.

Besides the campaigns that are launched to promote share issues every company needs to maintain a continuous flow of communications to and relations with existing shareholders. The function of communicating with the shareholders, sometimes also referred to as stockholders, has acquired considerable importance as the number of shareholders has grown and the complexities of the capital market have increased. Since this calls for special skills and a very thorough grasp of the factors that influence the investing public it has led some people in the profession to specialise in what is known as financial public relations. In some of the developed industrial countries even firms which have their own elaborate PR setups seek the help of financial public relations consultants when planning any major campaign aimed at this segment of the public. In India we have not reached that degree of specialisation but increasingly managements are beginning to except that relations with the capital market should be handled in a professional manner on a continuing basis. The publication of the annual report even though it still occupies and will continue to occupy an important place in the total communication mix to shareholders, is not the only medium for communication with the shareholders.

Annual Report

The Public Relations Department of a company does not have any direct responsibility for preparing the balance sheet and the sections relating to the accounts, auditors' report, directors' report, etc., but it should advise management on the overall approach of the Report, the theme of the Chairman's statement and also on the format and presentation of the Report.

Presently, there are at present certain statutory requirements about the information that an Annual Report must contain. These statutory provisions should be implemented not only in letter but in spirit. The main provisions are as follows:

The report shall be in respect of—

(a) the state of the company's affairs;
(b) the amounts, if any, which it proposes to carry to any reserves in such balance sheet;
(c) the amount, if any, which it recommends should be paid by way of dividend; and
(d) material changes and commitments, if any, affecting the financial position of the company which have occurred between the end of the financial year of the company to which the balance sheet relates and the date of the report.

It is also required that the report shall deal with any changes which have occurred during the financial year —

(a) in the nature of the company's business;
(b) in the company's subsidiaries or, in the nature of the business carried on by them; and
(c) generally in the classes of business in which the company has an interest.

The above information has to be given so far as it is material for the appreciation of the state of the company's affairs by its members and will not in the board's opinion be harmful to the business of the company.

The Board's report is also required to include a statement showing the name of every employee of the company, who—

(a) if employed throughout the financial year, was in receipt of remuneration for that year which, in the aggregate, was not less than thirty-six thousand rupees; or
(b) if employed for a part of the financial year, was in receipt of remuneration for any part of that year, at a rate which, in the aggregate, was not less than three thousand rupees per month.

The statement referred to above shall also indicate—

(a) whether any such employee is a relative of any director or manager of the company and if so, the name of such director; and
(b) such other particulars as are prescribed in the Companies (Particulars of Employees) Rules, 1975.

Regarding the balance sheet and profit-and-loss account and schedules and statements, these have to be set out in the forms given in Part I and II of Schedule VI of the Companies Act or as near thereto as circumstances permit or in such other form as may be approved by the Central Government.

Beside the information that is required to be given by law the report should try to give as complete a picture of the company as possible to the shareholders and the other financial publics. New products or processes developed during the year, new plants opened, new distribution centres established are some items of information that can usefully be given research and development is area of activity that should be highlighted especially if there is any significant achievement to be reported. Training and development of the human resources is also a feature of functioning that needs to be covered. It is also useful to compare figures relating to the current year's performance not only with the previous year but also in relation to a longer period spread over some years. This enables investors to get a picture of the company which a single year's or even two years results would not be able to impart. While a decision would have to be taken each year on what should be highlighted depending on the immediate objectives for the current year, and the particular public that requires to be reached, it would be well to remember that the impact is most effective if a single theme is chosen for each year's annual report. Trying to state too much and to cover too many areas of activity with equal emphasis only tends to diffuse the message with the result that it fails to create any impression. Many companies are following the practice of giving all the information statutorily required but in addition taking up one theme and highlighting the company's performance, plans and outlook in that particular area.

Illustrations certainly help and should preferably be given keeping in mind that the impact will be greater if the illustrations reinforce the main theme. A random collection of photographs, however good they may be individually, will tend to be ignored. If a single theme cannot be selected the effort should be to present a story that will link various facets of a company's activity which it is considered desirable to project. The use of colour always makes a better impact but this has to be balanced with the financial resources of the company. If a Company is small and has limited turnover and profit, using a large slice of it to present a multicoloured lavishly produced annual report would seriously annoy the shareholders. On the other hand, a large company with substantial turnover can afford to and is, in fact, expected to be more liberal with its spending on the Annual Report. But even for a large company to produce a very expensive report in a year when the profits have been low and the dividend to be declared is also low, would be extremely imprudent.

The Chairman's statement at the Annual General Meeting also deserves serious attention. Whether as is the practice with certain companies, it forms a part of the Annual Report or goes out separately to shareholders it is an important medium of communication which shareholders generally consider seriously. Together with the balance sheet and the Directors' report it provides an index of the financial stability and the future prospects of the company. Chairman's statements are, therefore, now-a-days being used to project the company image. Many companies, use the Chairman's statement not only to draw attention to the financial highlights of the year but to communicate some message of significance to the shareholders.

It is also the custom to publish the Chairman's statement in the newspapers, both those which deal in general news and those which specialise in financial affairs. This is a correct and sound practice because it gives an opportunity to project the company to a larger audience besides the company's own registered shareholders. However, in many cases this is done as a kind of ritual and no effort is made to derive the maximum advantage from this fairly costly exercise. Instead of presenting the statement, in small print in exactly the same form as it is printed in the Annual Report or the special folder that is sent out to shareholders, it increases the impact tremendously if the report is published in the creases the impact tremendously if the report is published in the newspapers with sketches and/or photographs with proper subheadings and an attractive headline. To avoid excessive expenditure the statement are emphasised which need to be and which convey the message to the audience that is of most significance to the company at that particular moment.

Apart from the registered shareholders, there are four other segments of the financial public which are important from the company's point of view. They are—

(a) the financial community including banks, the term lending institutions or the government financial institutions, stock brokers, etc.;

(b) the investing community generally, the potential shareholders who generally lookout for suitable companies to invest in;

(c) the business community in general.

(d) the financial press;

Based on the situation the company is being face and its short-term as well as long-term objectives, communication links should be established with each of the above-mentioned publics. This can be achieved through six monthly or quarterly reports, articles in the financial press reporting the progress of the company or by personal contact.

15

Content Analysis: Importance and Relevance

In every educative process — whether it be 'formal' or 'non-formal' — both 'matter' and 'method' are important. These may differ for different types of 'givers' and takers' (programmers', 'implementors,' 'executives,' 'performers' on the one hand and the 'beneficiaries' — 'listeners,' 'viewers' 'participants' — on the other). It is necessary to plan 'who' gives 'what' 'to whom' 'when' 'where' 'how' and 'for what' purpose. All these factors are equally important in any process of instruction or communication.

'Conscientisation' or 'creating awareness' has become an inevitable component of any action aimed at the welfare or development of people. In order to 'liberate' people from illiteracy, poverty, ill-health, lack of housing, superstitions, beliefs, customs, manners etc. we have to enter into a 'dialogue' with them, create an awareness and appropriate climate for action and thus help them liberate themselves through action. The 'messages' that are to be communicated have to be properly selected and conveyed for ensuring 'enrichment of knowledge and skills' and consequent attitudinal changes.' The needs, aspirations and anxieties of the masses have to be ascertianed before launching programme. Gandhiji has established his 'message' through his 'life.' India needs such leaders, but we rarely have such people in the contemporary world. It is easy to 'preach' but difficult to 'practise.' Hence messages should be communicated to people through such persons whom we could emulate as 'ideals.' The matter or message should be presented in such a way that it is appealing to those concerned. Multiple approaches are needed. Folk art forms and modern media have to be selectively and appropriately used.

Content analysis can refer to the past, present and future. When any book, programme or project that has been published or completed is analysed to ascertain the 'relevance of the content,' it can help in improving the same in future. Similar is the objective of a 'concurrent' analysis. But prior to launching a programme it is advisable to attempt a content analysis to ensure 'relevance and contemporaneity of the content. A survey, discussion, analysis etc. can lead to this. Experts, Practitioners and Planners should sit together discuss and finalise the content. When the area or topic covered is of an 'interdisciplinary' nature, this is all the more essential. Analysis of felt needs expressed through letters or in newspaper columns, or identified through surveys and expressed in seminars, conferences, corner meetings etc. can also serve the purpose.

Some Findings of the Evaluative Studies

Here are given the experiences of Trivandrum (Kerala) Kendra of Akashvani and Doordarshan.

In the evaluative study it was found that the following messages went deeper into the minds of the people:

Immunisation, Child welfare, Pregnancy and lactation, Balanced diet, Family welfare, Diarrhoea, Hygiene, Punctuality, Family planning, Superstitious, Physical handicaps.

There was demand for emphasising Pre School/Early childhood education and 'role of fathers' also in the programme. Rebraodcast of the programme in different forms, giving more time for 'question—answer' was also recommended based on opinions expressed.

Special appreciation was given to topics like Maternity care, Mental development of children, Habits of Children, Child and Environment, Immunisation and Pre Primary Education.

The major messages identified by the listeners were: Importance of breast feeding, Importance of family planning, Need for eradicating superstitious beliefs, Importance of immunisation, Care during pregnancy, Treatment of diarrhoea and prevention of deficiency diseases.

More emphasis was demanded on 'Health and Hygiene,' Mentally retarded children, Rights of the Child and Dental care.

Many favoured changing the title form 'Ammayum Kunjum' (Mother and Child) to Kunjum Kudumbavum' (Family and Child) covering children up to the age of 5 years, emphasising on 'Early Childhood Care and Education' (ECCE) and rebroadcast of the series.

This is an indication of the demand for the interest in such programmes through Radio and Television. Not only mothers, ICDS workers, Anganvadi personnel and Welfare workers demand this programme, but the public in general are eager to hear and view these programmes which are inevitable for the entire masses for ensuring better life for their children and themselves.

It is the responsibility of media personnel, through their Audience Research Unit or otherwise, on the needs, desires and demands of the people and provide for, within their limitations and constraints.

Summing Up

The change in topics covered in the 26 broadcasts of "Mother and Child' (in 1988 and 1990) by AIR, Trivandrum station (as depicted separately) is itself ample proof for pre and post content analysis. It is not enough if we identify the content topic or area—properly, it is equally important to present the same in the best manner possible. In order to avoid factual errors and to ensure most up to date information subject experts have to be consulted. Their scripts may be transformed into a variety of presentable forms by media personnel to make the broadcast/telecast, attractive, easily understandable and message-conveying so that `attitudinal and behavioural changes' can emerge. Care should be taken to ensure 'accuracy' of content and messages at a joint meting of subject experts and media people. Priority and weightage for various content units also have to be work out scientifically. It should be noted that "the contents of education (or programme) should be relevant to the `business of living' and `making a living' and should `enable people to adjust themselves to their environments.' Topics for study (or discussion) should `spring from the environment' and be `intimately related to the problems of everyday life." Hence the main concern of the programmers should be to make the content (subject matter or topic) `relevant to the present and future needs of the community' at large and with special reference to the target groups concerned or identified.

Definitely, the cited instance of Public Relations in the area of child and mother care, proves that content analysis of any programme of utmost use.

16

Public Relations for Marketing

In the field of marketing and customer care Public Relations is of vital importance. In the 21st century when globalisation is a boom its importance, has increased manifold. According its strategy has become more complex.

Public Relations can be an aid to marketing all along the line from the planning of a new product to its effective selling. Public Relations will help to evaluate customer attitudes towards a product and the company producing it. From this evaluation may emerge important clues for the marketing team which will help it to decide whether to continue with the product or a product line or to modify the product or, if necessary, even to drop the product altogether and go in for a new one. Public Relations helps to give the right orientation not only to the sales force but to all employees within an organisation—those who make the product, those who test it, those who package and despatch it and those who sell and service it. In some organisations a wrong attitude on the part of the employees drives away customers even when the product is good.

A sales campaign has thus often to begin with an internal communication campaign within the company—a, campaign that can most effectively be conducted by the Public Relations department. Again left to themselves the sales force of a company might be content with just selling the product. Except for certain sophisticated varieties of equipment and machinery after sales service would probably be regarded as an unnecessary item of expenditure. Public Relations helps organisations to realise that winning customer goodwill on a long-term basis is a worthwhile investment which will pay dividends in the long-run even if it reduces the margin of profit slightly in the short-run.

Customer Complaints

Customer complaints attending is one more important aspect of Public Relations for marketing. No organisation which is interested in securing customer goodwill can afford to neglect customer complaints. There should be some standing arrangements in any organisation to handle them, preferably as a part of the marketing apparatus of the organisation. .However, the Public Relations department will have to be closely involved also because consumer complaints often have an impact on a wider public. They may take the form of a letter to the editor of a newspaper or give rise to a question in the Parliament or the State Legislature. Consumer complaints need to be dealt with promptly. If a complaint takes the form of a letter in writing to the firm it should be acknowledged immediately with a promise to investigate the whole matter.

After investigation which should be carried out impartially by some responsible member of the management team remedial measures should be worked out. One should remember that within the organisation there is often a tendency to cover up failures and all effort therefore will have to be made to ferret out the truth. If on investigation the customer complaint is found to be groundless or frivolous, a polite letter, explaining the position should be sent. On no account should rude letters be written or the management betray impatience even if the customer is patently at fault. On the other hand if the company has really been at fault steps kind of an apology combined with certain remedial steps which may consist of an offer to replace or repair the product at fault should be sent instantly.

In case of a complaint finding its way into the newspapers a rejoinder would have to be sent. If it has become a subject of discussion in the Parliament or State Legislature or local municipal body a letter may be sent to the press clarifying the situation or letters-may be sent to the members who have raised the question explaining the facts as the company sees them. In all cases there should be no hesitation in admitting lapses or failures if there have been any. Trying to hide the truth or explain away the lapses will only make matters worse.

In Launching a New Product

Well in advance the product is ready for the launch a meeting of the three teams should be organised to work out the timetable and the action plan for the launch indicating clearly the action points for each of the teams and the dates within which the takes allotted to each of them have to be completed. The action plan will involve a period for internal preparation and internal communication.

In the internal communication programme the Public Relations department would normally be expected to play a part either by publishing a feature in the house journal or issuing some kind of internal communication folder or by arranging for some sort of audiovisual communication. Where complex problems fare likely to come up and detailed discussions are necessary to ensure that all points are clarified, some sort of internal seminar may be arranged. The Public Relations department will also have to arrange the publication of sales literature, point of sales material instruction manual for the use of the product and also develop an advertising campaign. The advertising may involve use of one or more media, such as newspaper, radio, outdoor, TV, etc. If the type of product that has been developed justifies it, a press conference may be called to launch the product. In other cases a press release may suffice. In still other cases it may be felt that the product is suitable for projection only through advertising. If the advertising campaign involves a coupon response the Public Relations department may be asked to handle the coupons and mail out the replies. It is, however, generally better to leave that to the marketing team as this is more directly related to the marketing function. In any case it is essential that if a coupon response is a part of the advertising campaign adequate arrangements should be made before launching the campaign to deal with the coupons that come in.

'Exhibition' is yet another medium for product publicity. This is particularly suited to products that require demonstration such as consumer durables or an industrial product such as a machine. The organisation of the display of the company's products in exhibitions and trade fairs is normally a function of the Public Relations.

Customer Publications

A very effective form of public relations is the publication of journals which carry articles feature and news to the industry to which the product is related. Thus a tyre manufacturer may have a journal on the automobile industry, an electrode manufacturer on the welding industry or the engineering industry. Such journals are often not just publicity brochures cataloguing the company's products but contain news and articles of interest to all those connected with the industry. They are thus read by the people in the profession and create goodwill for the product. Readers of the company's journal if they are impressed by it naturally develop a preference for the products manufactured by the company.

Sponsored Programme

Sponsored programmes on radio or TV are a form of Public Relations for marketing that can often prove quite effective. On the commercial channel of All India Radio there are quite a few examples of sponsored programmes, many of which have achieved very considerable listener interest. Examples of sponsored programmes on TV are too numerous to need citing. Another interesting form that Public Relations for marketing can take is the organisation of fashion shows—a form that is normally adopted by manufacturers of textiles or by women's magazines or sometimes by the two in collaboration.

REFERENCES

Kolter, Philip *Marketing Management Analysis, Planning and Control,* Prentice Hall of India (Pvt.) Ltd., New Delhi..

Rotman, Morris B. (1974), *'PR is Still Necessary Adjunct to Efficient Marketing Today'* Advertising & Sales Promotion.

Mehta, D.S. (1992), "A Public Relations fob" *Hindustan Times,* Sunday-Supplement.

Seitel, Fraser P. Charles E., *The Practice of Public Relations,* Merrill Publishing Co. A Bell & Howell Company, Columbus.

17

Public Relations in Extension

The practice of creating, promoting or maintaining goodwill and a favourable image among the public towards an institution or public body is conventionally known as public relations. Basically, success of Public Relations depends on the communication method adopted.

The choice of a channel or method of communication, also known as extension teaching method, generally depends on the number of location of the target audience and the time available for communication. They are categorised as individual method, group method and mass method. Each of the methods has both advantages and limitations. The extension worker has to choose a particular method or combination of methods according to the needs of the situation.

Mainly, three methods are used in extension teaching.

1. INDIVIDUAL METHOD

The extension worker communicates with the people individually, maintaining separate identity of each person. This method is applicable and followed when the number of people to be contacted are few, are conveniently located close to the communicator, and sufficient time is available for communication work. The main merits and limitations of this method are as follows.

Merits

(i) It helps the extension worker in building rapport.

(ii) It facilitates gaining first hand knowledge of farm and home.

(iii) It helps in selecting demonstrators and local leaders.

(iv) It helps in teaching complex practices.

(v) It helps in changing attitude of the .people.

(vi) Enhances effectiveness of group and mass methods.

(vii) Facilitates getting feedback information.

Limitations

(i) This method is time consuming and relatively expensive.

(ii) This has low coverage of audience.

(iii) Extension worker may develop favouritism or bias towards some persons.

Types of Individual Methods

1. Farm and Home Visit

Farm and Home Visit is a direct, face-to-face contact by the extension worker with the farmer or homemaker at their farm or home for extension work.

Objectives

(i) To get acquainted with a gain confidence of farmers and homemakers.

(ii) To obtain and/or give firsthand information on matters relating to farm and home.

(iii) To advice and assist in solving specific problems, and teach skills.

(iv) To sustain interest.

Techniques Used

Planning and Preparation

(i) Decide on the audience and the objective—whom to meet and what for?

(ii) Get adequate information about the topic. Contact research if needed.

(iii) Collect relevant publications and materials to be handed over.

(iv) Make a schedule of visits to save time and energy.

(v) If possible, send advance information.

Implementation

(i) Visit on the scheduled date and time or according to convenience of the farmer and when he is likely to listen.

(ii) Create interest of the farmer and allow him to talk first.

(iii) Present your message or points of view and explain up to the satisfaction of the farmer.

(iv) Answer to questions raised and clarify doubts. Handover publications.

(v) Try to get some assurance for action.

Follow-up

(i) Keep appropriate record of the visit.

(ii) Send any further information or material for which commitment has been made.

(iii) Make subsequent visit as and when necessary.

Limitations

(i) Only limited number of contracts may be made.

(ii) Time consuming and costly method.

(iii) Attention may be concentrated on a few big and

progressive persons; neglecting the large number of small, marginal, tribal farmers, landless labour and backward people; which may prejudice them.

2. Office Call

Office Call is a call made by a farmer or homemaker at the office of the extension worker for obtaining information and assistance.

Objectives

(i) To get quick solution of problems relating to farm and home.
(ii) To enable the farmer and homemaker to bring specimens for proper identification of the problem.
(iii) To ensure timely supply of inputs and services.
(iv) To act as a reminder to the extension worker.

Techniques Used

Planing and Preparation

(i) Extension worker shall remain present in the office on fixed days and hours, which have been communicated to the farmers and homemakers in advance.
(ii) Extension worker shall make alternative arrangements to provide information and assistance to the caller in his absence.
(iii) Extension worker shall organise an information centre in the office or at least put up a few boards in his room and display current leaflets, folders, photographs, charts etc.

Implementation

(i) Allow the visitor to talk first and make his point.
(ii) Discuss about his problems and prescribe solutions. If necessary, take him to the subject matter specialist.

(iii) Let the visitor leave the office satisfied.

Follow-up

(i) Make a note of the call, if necessary.

(ii) If required, refer the problem to research for solution.

(iii) Supply further information and materials if such commitment has been made.

Limitations

(i) Being away from the situation, it may be difficult for the extension worker to understand the problem in its proper perspective.

(ii) Extension worker may not be available all the time.

3. Personal Letter

Personnal Letter is written by the extension worker to particular farmers or homemakers in connection with extension work.

Objectives

(i) To answer to queries relating to problems of farm and home.

(ii) To send information or seek cooperation on important extension activities.

Techniques Used

(i) Send the letter in time, or if a letter has already been received, send a prompt reply.

(ii) The content should be clear, complete, to the point and applicable to farmer's own situation.

(iii) Use simple and courteous language.

4. Minikit Trial in Individual Farm and Home

Adaptive or Minikit Trial is a method of determining the suitability or otherwise of a new practice in farmer's situation. This is the first stage a new and improved practice passes through, before it is taken up for result or method demonstration or recommended for large scale adoption.

On-farm trials are not meant to try to simulate experiment station conditions in farmers' fields. Rather, they are designed to help detect differences under typical farmer management practices and environmental conditions. This is a crucial first step in making recommendations that are appropriate for the farmers. The broad objectives being: (a) To test a new and promising practice under the resources, constraints and abilities of the farmer; (b) To find out the profitability of the new practice in comparison to the existing one; (c) To build up confidence of the extension workers, research workers and farmers; (d) To act as a precaution against insignificant, faulty or hasty recommendations.

Techniques Used

Planning and Preparation

(i) Select promising practices suitable for the area in consultation with research and farmers.

(ii) Select a small number of innovative farmers.

Implementation

(i) Explain the objective to the demonstrating farmers. Make it clear that it is a trial and does not involve great risk.

(ii) Supply the critical inputs in time and supervise all important operations or steps personally.

(iii) Assist the farmer to maintain accurate records.

2. GROUP METHOD

Contrary to individual method, in this method, the extension worker communicates with the people in groups and not as individual persons. This method is applied when it is necessary to communicate with a number of people simultaneously, who are located not far off from the communicator, and reasonably good time is available for communication.

There may be a few communicators such as the extension worker and some subject matter specialists. The size of a small group may be from 15 to 25, a medium group from 25 to 50 while a large group from 50 to 100 persons. Examples of group method are result demonstration, method demonstration, group meeting, small group training, field visit, study tour etc.

The following are the main advantages and limitations of this method:

Advantages

(i) This may anable a extension worker to have face-to-face contact with a number of people at a time.

(ii) A select part of the target group.

(iii) Knowledge and experience sharing and solid learning of the group members can be facilitated .

(iv) Reach fewer farmers, but offer more opportunities for interaction and feedback.

(v) Satisfies the basic urge of people for social contacts.

(vi) Motivate people to accept change due to group influence.

(vii) More effective than mass method in stimulating action.

(viii) Less expensive than individual method due to more coverage.

Limitations

(i) Wide diversity in the interest of group members may create a difficult learning situation.

(ii) Holding the meeting may be regarded as the objective in itself.

(iii) Vested interests, caste groups and village factions may hinder free interaction and decision making by the group members.

Types of Group Methods

1. Result Demonstration

Result Demonstration is a method of motivating the people for adoption of a new practice by showing its distinctly superior result. The demonstrations are conducted in the farm or home of selected individuals and are utilised to educate and motivate groups of people in their neighbourhood. This is a very effective method for the transfer of technology in a community.

Demonstrations may stimulate farmers to try out innovations themselves, or even may replace a test of the innovation by the farmer. They can show the causes of problems and their possible solutions without complicated technical details. A great advantage of demonstration is seeing how an innovation works in practice. This shall encourage the farmers to act on the basis of scientific view, rather than something which is magical. Demonstrations, to be effective, should be well integrated with the total extension programme.

Techniques Used

Planning and Preparation

(i) Analyse farmers' situation and select relevant profitable practices, in consultation with research and farmers.

(ii) Select a few responsible and cooperating farmers having adequate resources and facilities and having acceptance in the local community for conducting the demonstration. This, however, does not mean that big farmers are to be selected.

(iii) Select representative locations for conducting the demonstrations where it will be easily visible to a large number of people in the community.

(iv) It may be a good practice to have at least two demonstrations in different parts of the village or on farms of different sizes.

(v) Prepare a calendar of operations.

Implementation

(i) Explain the objectives and steps to the demonstrating farmers.

(ii) Organise materials and equipments necessary for conducting the demonstrations.

(iii) Give adequate publicity about the demonstrations.

(iv) Start the demonstrations on the scheduled date and time, in front of those who may be present. Explain the objectives to those who are present.

(v) Arrange method demonstration where a new skill is involved.

(vi) Put up suitable signboard for each demonstration in prominent places.

(vii) Ensure that all critical operations are done in time and try to supervise them personally.

(viii) Conduct field day or field visit of interested farmers around successful demonstrations.

(ix) Take photographs. Help the demonstrating farmers to maintain records.

(x) Motivate as many farmers as possible to remain present at the time of final assessment of the result.

(xi) Let the demonstrating farmers explain to the visitors as far as possible.

(xii) Analyse and interpret the data, and compare them with the farmers' existing practice.

(xiii) Emphasise applicability of the new practice in the farmers' own situation.

Follow-up

(i) Use the result of the demonstrations in future extension work and also pass on to the mass media for further dissemination.

(ii) Utilise demonstrating farmers in farmers' meetings and training programmes.

(iii) Prepare visual aids, particularly photographs, coloured slides, charts etc. on the demonstrations.

(iv) Avoid conducting subsequent demonstrations with the same farmers.

Limitations

(i) Need more time, energy and funds for extension work.

(ii) Unsuccessful demonstrations may cause some setback in extension work.

2. Method Demonstration

It is essentially a skill training, where the emphasis involves seeing, hearing, participating and practicing in a group which shall stimulate interest and action. Method demonstration is sometimes used as complementary to result demonstration.

Objectives

(i) To teach skills and stimulate people to action.

(ii) To get rid of inefficient or inefficient or ineffective movements.

(iii) To improve upon the result by doing a job in a better way.

(iv) To build up learners' confidence and satisfaction on the practice.

Techniques Used

Planning and Preparation

(i) Decide on the topic, target audience and venue of demonstration.

(ii) Select a topic which is important and needed by the participants for immediate use.

(iii) Contact subject matter specialists and ensure their participation.

(iv) Collect relevant information, materials and equipments.

(v) Identify the steps in conducting the demonstration. Practise the demonstration, to be sure about its correct presentation within the allotted time.

(vi) Decide on the date and time in consultation with the local leaders and give timely intimation to all concerned.

(vii) Complete all arrangements for the demonstration.

(viii) Display diagrams, charts, graphs etc. at the demonstration site.

Implementation

(i) Start the demonstration on the scheduled date and time.

(ii) Show each operation step-by-step, explaining clearly why and how it is being done.

(iii) Ensure that all the participants have seen the demonstration. Repeat difficult steps, if required.

(iv) Invite the participants one by one or in small

batches to practice the skill. Clarify doubts and answer to their questions.

(vi) Hand over the relevant publications.

Follow-up

(i) Keep a record of the participants and maintain contact with them through field staff and personal visit.

(ii) Assist the participants in getting the required materials and equipments.

Limitations

(i) Suitable only for practices involving skills.

(ii) Needs good deal of preparation, equipments and skill of the extension worker.

(iii) May require transportation of materials and equipments.

(iv) Requires some amount of showmanship which may not be possessed by some extension workers.

3. Group Meeting

Group Meeting is a method of democratically arriving at certain decisions by a group, by taking into consideration the members' points of view. The convenient size of a group for conducting a meeting or discussion may be around 15 to 25, which may be extended up to about 50.

Group discussion is a very important extension method, as it provides opportunity to influence the participants' behaviour. Group discussion can play an important role in increasing knowledge and changing attitude, as well as in changing behaviour. It provides a means of two-way communication between the extension worker and subject matter specialists on the one hand and the participants on the other. It helps in collective decision making.

Objectives

(i) To prepare a favourable climate for discussion and help in better understanding of the problem by pooling the knowledge and experience of a number of persons.

(ii) To facilitate in-depth discussion by involving a small number of participants.

(iii) To generate new ideas and methods and select the rational ones through group interaction.

(iv) To develop a favourable attitude and commitment for action through group involvement.

(v) To act as a safety valve for reducing tension.

Technique

Planning and Preparation

(i) Decide on the topic to be discussed and the persons to be involved.

(ii) Collect relevant informations. Contact research, if required.

(iii) May request subject matter specialists to participate in the meeting.

Implementation

(i) Start the meeting on the scheduled date and time.

(ii) Introduce the topic to the group and initiate discussion.

(iii) Allow the members to talk and interact.

(iv) Facilitate discussion by further explaining the points already made and giving new points, if required.

(v) Assist the less vocal members to participate.

(vi) Encourage the group to take decisions and make a record of important decisions arrived at.

Follow-up

(i) Remind the members of the decisions, and encourage and assist them to take action.

(ii) Arrange inputs including credit.

(iii) Sustain interest through personal contact.

Limitations

(i) Requires understanding of group dynamics and skill of the extension worker.

(ii) Village factions may hinder successful use of this method.

(iii) Group members must have some self-discipline.

(iv) A slow process and unsuitable in crisis and emergency situation.

4. Small Group Training

Small Group Training is a technique of imparting specific skills to a group of people who need them by creating appropriate learning situation. This is an effective method for transfer of technology in a community.

Objectives

(i) To impart the needed skills to a small group of people.

(ii) To motivate people to adopt new practices through skill training.

Technique

Planning and Preparation

(i) Identify a suitable technology for the group for which there is a need.

(ii) Decide on the time and duration of the training programme.

(iii) Select appropriate speakers and ensure their participation. The speakers should have both theoretical knowledge and practical experience about the technology.
(iv) Prepare a written programme allocating topics to different speakers.
(v) Collect relevant materials, publications and audio-visual aids.
(vi) Inform all concerned in time.
(vii) Make arrangements for food, accommodation etc.
(viii) Allocate responsibilities to suitable persons.
(ix) Make arrangement for registration of the participations.

Implementation

(i) Start the training programme on the appointed date and time.
(ii) Distribute publications, pad or note book and a pencil or dot pen.

Objectives

(i) To expose the visitors to a new and different situation which shall help in changing their outlook and extend their mental horizon.
(ii) To understand the gap in technology adoption.
(iii) To explore the feasibility of adopting new practices in visitors' own situations.
(iv) To induce a spirit of competition amongst the participants by showing what others have been able to achieve.

Techniques Used

Planning and Preparation

(i) Decide on the objective, number and type of participants, duration and places of visit.

(ii) Make correspondence well in advance and get confirmation of the programme, accommodation etc.
(iii) Discuss with the participants and finalise the travel plan.
(iv) Make a meaningful programme, which is compact, but not crowded. Allow some loose time to cope with unforeseen situations.
(v) Arrange for conveyance, tickets etc.
(vi) Communicate the programme in writing to all concerned and ask them to report in time at the appointed place.

Implementation

(i) Keep the interest of the group uppermost in mind.
(ii) Let everyone see, hear, discuss, and if possible participate in the activities at the places of visit.
(iii) In case of language barrier act as an interpreter.
(iv) Allow time for question and answers.
(v) Çollect publications for the participants and help them to take note of interesting and useful information.
(vi) Take photographs of study tour.
(vii) Avoid changes in the programme unless otherwise necessary.
(viii) If possible, send one staff member in advance to the next place of visit to check up all arrangements.
(ix) Provide for recreation and sight seeing. Look to the comfort and safety of the group.
(x) Let the representatives of the group share the responsibility for food, finance, recreation and maintenance of accounts etc.

Follow-up

(i) Keep contact with the participants through field staff and personal visit.

(ii) Encourage adoption of practices by arranging necessary supply and service.

(iii) Buildup news stories.

Limitations

(i) Because of limitations of funds and time, study tours can not be held frequently.

(ii) There may be some possibility of subordinating educational aspect to sight and recreation.

(iii) Unpleasant experience may cause a setback.

3. MASS METHOD

This method is followed where a large and widely dispersed audience is to be communicated within a short time. There may be a few communicators such as the extension worker and some subject matter specialists. The size of the audience may be a few hundreds in mass meeting, few thousands in campaign and exhibition and millions in newspaper, radio and television.

The main advantages and limitation of this method are:

Advantages

(i) Suitable for creating general awareness amongst the people.

(ii) Helps in transferring knowledge and, forming and changing opinions.

(iii) Large number of people may be communicated within a short time.

(iv) Facilitates quick communication in times of emergency.

(v) Reinforces previous learning.

(vi) Less expensive due to more coverage.

Limitations

(i) A less intensive method.

(ii) Little scope of extension worker for personal contact with the audience.

(iii) Little opportunity for interaction amongst the audience.

(iv) Generalised recommendations hinder application by individuals.

(v) Little control by the extension worker over the responses of the audience.

(vi) Difficulty in getting feedback information and evaluation of results.

Types of Mass Methods

1. Farm Publication

Farm Publication is a class of publications prepared by the extension agency in printed form, containing informations relating to the improvement of farm and home. Farm publications may be used singly or in combination with other extension methods. Farm publications are of various types such as leaflet, folder, bulletin, newsletter, journal and magazine.

Leaflet. It is a single printed sheet of paper of small size, containing preliminary information relating to a topic. It is made as and when needed. Generally distributed free-of-cost.

Folder. It is a single printed sheet of paper of big size, folded once or twice, and gives essential information relating to a particular topic. It is printed as and when required. Generally distributed free-of-cost.

Bulletin. It is printed, bound booklet with a number of

pages, containing complete information in respect to a particular topic. It is made as and when necessary. A small price may be fixed on some important bulletins.

Newsletter. It is miniature newspaper in good quality paper, containing information relating to the activities and achievements of the organisation. It has fixed periodicity of publication. Generally distributed free-of-cost.

Journal, magazine. It is a periodical, containing information related to various topics of interest not only for the farmers but also for the extension workers. It has a fixed periodicity of publication. Generally supplied against pre-payment of subscription for a particular period.

Farm publications are extremely useful to the literate farmers. Even illiterate farmers can make use of them with the help of literate members in their family. Farm publications are used by all types of extension functionaries, in the field including bank personnel and mediamen in the newspapers, radio and television. These may be used in most of the individual, group and mass methods.

Objectives

(i) To reach a large number of people quickly and simultaneously at low cost.

(ii) To provide accurate, motivating, credible and distortion—free information.

(iii) To provide support to other extension methods.

(iv) To facilitate use at convenience and to serve as a future reference.

Technique

Planning and Preparation

(i) Select a topic of economic and practical importance, for which information is needed by the audience.

(ii) Estimate the time required to prepare, print and despatch, and plan the publication in such a way that it reaches the audience in time.

(iii) Check up availability of funds and decide on the number of copies to be printed. It may be useful to have more copies at less cost, than a few copies at high cost.

Implementation

(i) Collect relevant information on the topic from all available sources.

(ii) Contact specialists relating to all relevant disciplines.

(iii) Prepare the draft in clear, simple, short and direct sentences, keeping the target audience in view. Avoid using text book language.

(iv) Arrange in short paragraphs, in a logical sequence.

(v) Give suitable title to the publication and sub-heads to the paragraphs.

(vi) Devote the first paragraph in highlighting the economic and other advantages. Print this in bold letter.

(vii) Present all weights and measures clearly and directly. For example, instead of writing percentage of a solution, write how much quantity of the material is to be added to a unit quantity of water.

(viii) Revise the draft twice or thrice, keeping an eye on Accuracy, Brevity and Clarity (ABC are fundamental to all good writing). Revise the draft with the specialists also. Avoid writing more than what is necessary.

(ix) A write-up for the farmers may be pre-tested with sample farmers which shall enhance its understandability.

(x) Below the press line put the name of the department and the organisation under whose authority it is being published. Acknowledge assistance of departments and scientists who have made significant contribution. Give the name and address of the printing press, year of publication and number of copies printed.

(xi) Select suitable photograph and diagrams and indicate where these are to be placed.

(xii) Prepare the manuscript on one side of the paper and send it to the printing press with necessary instructions for layout, design, colour, size, quality of paper etc.

(xiii) Correct the proof at least thrice and ensure that there is not a single mistake in the publication.

(xiv) Be in close personal contact with the press and get the publication printed according to your liking. Consider suggestions given by the press.

Follow-up

(i) Arrange timely despatch of the publication to the target audience and for the extension programmes.

(ii) Despatch to the media-men and others according to mailing list.

(iii) Attend to requests for publications promptly.

(iv) Try to get feedback information from the users.

(v) Keep surplus publications in convenient packers suitably labelled. Store them in a dry and relatively dark place.

(vi) Maintain appropriate records for distribution and sale of publications.

Limitations

(i) Can not be widely used in areas of low level of literacy.

(ii) May lose its significance if not carefully prepared and used.

(iii) Periodical revision is necessary to keep the publication up-to-date.

2. Mass Meeting

Mass Meeting is held to communicate interesting and useful information to a large audience at a time. The size of the audience for mass meeting may be a few hundreds, but at the time of *melas* or festivals it may be few thousands. The majority of the audience have a purpose in attending the meeting, though some outsiders may attend it out of curiosity. Mass meeting may be held in a covered or in an open place. Public address system is essential for conducting mass meeting. Slide or film show may enhance effectiveness of the meeting.

Objectives

(i) To focus attention of the people on some important aspect.

(ii) To create general awareness about a programme or project and to announce its progress.

(iii) To enlist people's participation in community work.

(iv) To appear personally before a large audience.

Technique

Planning and Preparation

(i) Decide on the topic, occasion and the audience.

(ii) Select a limited number of speakers, including one or two local leaders, and ensure their participation.

(iii) Decide with the local leaders on the venue, date and time and communicate the same to all concerned well in advance.

(iv) Procure audio-visual aids, publications etc. and complete all arrangements at the site.

(v) Prepare a written programme of the meeting and distribute work to suitable persons.

Implementation

(i) Select a suitable chair-person.

(ii) Start the meeting in time and cut down the formalities to a minimum.

(iii) Focus attention to the central theme and do not allow any digression.

(iv) Prevent speech-making and keep the meeting moving on schedule.

(v) Use appropriate audio-visual aids where necessary.

(vi) Watch reaction of the audience. Encourage audience participation when desirable.

(vii) At appropriate time, take action on matters calling for decision.

(viii) Take advantage of group psychology and employ appeals that arouse interest, create desire and stimulate action.

(ix) Close the meeting in time with a brief summary by the chair-person.

(x) Give recognition to individuals and groups who have actively participated and helped.

(xi) Distribute relevant publications.

(xii) Take names of those interested in further information or follow-up.

Follow-up

(i) Establish contact with the interested persons through field staff and personal visit.

(ii) Sustain interest through mass media.

Limitations

(i) In-depth discussion of the topic not possible.
(ii) Can not be held frequently.
(iii) May be difficult to organise due to limited manpower, resources and facilities.
(iv) Difficult to get feedback information.

3. Exhibition

This method is suitable for reaching all types of people. Exhibitions may be held at the village, block sub-division, district, State, national and international levels. Through an exhibition is organised around a major theme, other related themes and some unrelated items like entertainment may also be included. Farmers' fairs and *Krishi melas* held by the agricultural universities, institutes and various other organisations in which field visit, training programmes etc. are combined with exhibition are effective and popular. Exhibitions may also be organised by taking advantage of local fairs and festivals. Exhibition aims at: (a) to acquaint people with better standards; (b) to create interest in a wide range of people; and (c) to motivate people to adopt better practices.

Techniques Used

Planning and Preparation

(i) Form a Steering Committee and suitable sub-committees with the specialists, local leaders and administrators.
(ii) Decide on the theme and the organisations to be involved.
(iii) Prepare a budget estimate and procure funds.
(iv) Decide on the venue, time and duration.
(v) Prepare a written programme and communicate to all concerned in time. Keep some recreational programmes in the evening.

(vi) Get the site ready within the scheduled date. Make provision for essential facilities.

(vii) Earmark a stall for display of exhibits to be brought by the farmers.

(viii) Arrange a pandal for holding meeting, training and entertainment programmes.

(ix) Display posters at important places. Publicize about the exhibition through mass media.

(x) Decorate the stalls simply and tastefully. Make adequate arrangements for lighting. Use special-effect light where necessary.

(xi) Prepare good quality and colourful exhibits which shall convey the desired message to the visitors. Use local materials as far as possible. Label the exhibits in local language with bold letters.

(xii) Display exhibits about 50 to 60 cm. above the floor of the stall, upto a height of about 2 meters. Maintain proper sequence. Avoid overcrowding of exhibits.

(xiii) If possible, arrange action and live exhibits.

(xiv) Train up interpreters and allot specific duties. For a long duration exhibition, arrange rotation and replacement of personnel.

Implementation

(i) Organise formal opening of the exhibition by a local leader or a prominent person.

(ii) Arrange smooth flow of visitors.

(iii) Let the interpreters briefly explain the exhibits to the visitors so that the intended message is clearly communicated.

(iv) Distribute publications during visit.

(v) Organise a panel of scientists to be present nearby, so that the visitors who would like to know more or discuss some problems could get the desired information.

(vi) Conduct meetings, training programmes etc. as per schedule during the day time.

(vii) Arrange judging of exhibits brought by the farmers and give away prizes and certificates.

(viii) Keep the exhibits and the premises clean. Replace exhibits as and when necessary.

Limitations

(i) Require lots of funds and preparation.

(ii) Can not be frequently held.

4. Campaign

A campaign is an intense education activity for motivating and mobilising a community to action, to solve a problem or satisfy a need urgently felt by it. The duration of a campaign may be for a few weeks as in rat control or family planning, for a few months as in vanamahotsava and for a few years as in 'Grow More Food' campaign. A campaign may be held by involving a small number of people in a few villages, or by involving an entire community or the entire nation over the whole country. Campaign around the theme may be organised only once, or may be repeated year after year, till the goal is satisfactorily reached. Campaign on a certain theme (say, environment) may be organised over the whole world.

Objectives

(i) To create mass awareness about an important problem or felt need of the community and encourage them to solve it.

(ii) To induce emotional participation of the community at the local level and create a favourable psychological climate for adoption of new practices.

Technique

Planning and Preparation

(i) Identify with the local leaders important problem or need of the community and how to tackle it.

(ii) List out specialists, local leaders and other persons to be involved and ensure their participation.

(iii) Decide with the local leaders about the time of holding the campaign and its duration.

(iv) Average necessary inputs, services and transport.

(v) Prepare a written programme of the campaign, clearly stating who will do what, and the phases it will pass through.

(vi) Give wide publicity and put up posters at strategic points throughout the area. Use mass media to warm up the community.

Implementation

(i) Carry out the campaign as per programme.

(ii) Hold group meeting with the people.

(iii) Arrange method demonstration where needed.

(iv) Maintain supply of critical inputs and services.

(v) Keep close watch on the campaign and take corrective steps, if necessary.

(vi) Arrange mass media coverage.

(vii) Conclude the campaign in time.

Follow-up

(i) Make individual and group contacts and find out reaction of the participants.

(ii) Assess the extent of adoption of the practice.

(iii) Publicise successful campaigns.

(iv) Analyse deficiencies and failures.

(v) Give due recognition to the local leaders.

Limitations

(i) Applicable only for topics of community interest.

(ii) Success depends on cooperation of the community and their leaders.

(iii) Unsuitable for practices involving complicated technicalities.

(iv) Requires adequate preparation of officials and non-officials, concerted efforts and propaganda techniques and uninterrupted supply of critical inputs.

5. Newspaper

Daily newspapers are resource-strong and are published from State capitals or big cities. Their approach is cosmopolitan and the circulation may range from less than a lakh to several lakhs. Some of the daily newspapers are quite big and are published simultaneously from a number of centres.

Small newspapers, on the other hand, are resource-weak and are published at weekly or fortnightly intervals, generally from the sub-divisional or district headquarters. These are local-oriented in approach limited circulation to a few thousands. Small newspapers, however, fill up some gap in communication which remains uncovered by the daily newspapers in the rural areas.

Behrens and Evans (1984) mentioned six ingredients which determine the news-worthiness of an information. Following them, they are: (i) *Timeliness*—The more timely the information, the greater is the news value; (ii) *Nearness*—The closer the information seems to the reader, geographically and psychologically, the greater is its news value; (iii) *Consequence*—The more the readers are affected by the information, the greater is its news value. (iv)

Human interest—Informations concerning human interest elements such as new programmes, personal involvement, profitability, progress etc. have more news value; (v) *Prominence*—Prominent people, places, things, events carry more news values; and (vi) *Editorial policy*—The editorial policy of a newspaper broadly determines the kinds and amounts of information it publishes.

Writing for the Newspapers

(i) Prepare a draft write-up in simple language, furnishing only the most important informations. The 'lead' i.e. the opening sentence or the opening paragraph is most important, and should be very comprehensive.

(ii) The draft should contain information on what, who, when, where any why.

(iii) Focus achievements in one or two sentences.

(iv) Give a suitable caption.

(v) Revise the draft and produce a brief, lucid, interesting and informative write-up.

(vi) If required, enclose photographs on glossy paper or block while sending the write-up to the newspaper.

Limitations

(i) Only literate people in general can take advantage of this medium.

(ii) Increase in the price of newspapers may restrict their circulation.

6. Radio

Radio is suitable for creating general awareness amongst the people, buildup desirable change in attitude and reinforce learning. The medium is extremely convenient for communication in times of crisis and urgent situation. People with no education or very little education and those who are to in a position to attend extension programmes personally, can take full advantage of this medium and build up adequate knowledge and skill. It reaches a large number of people at a very low cost. The programmes may be listened while one is engaged in farming our household work. The accessibility to farm radio, however, depends on the extent of radio ownership, the reception of radio signals, understandability of the message and convenience of listening time.

Rural and Farm Broadcasting

Baruah (1983) is of the opinion that the vast changes that have taken place in the countryside, particularly the 'green revolution' could not have come about so quickly without the use of radio. The educational and developmental role of radio has bene nowhere more evident than in its programmes for rural listeners. The AIR has played a significant part in bringing the new technology in agriculture to the door of the farmers by giving support to various farmers' training and functional literacy programmes of the Ministries of Agriculture and Education. In fact, the Farm and Home Units of *Akasvani* were started in 1966 to support the Intensive Agricultural District Programme and the coming of the new 'wonder' seeds—the high yielding varieties.

The objectives of Farm and Home broadcasts were two-fold: (a) to broadcast technical information on a continuing basis in alignment with the package of practices in respect of important crops of a particular area along with the information about services, and (b) to inform and educate the rural women on their efficient partnership in this process of change from traditional to modern farming and modern home making in line with the overall objective of Intensive Agricultural District Programme.

With the coming of scientific agriculture, continued reliance on radio for quick guidance and solution of problems became inevitable. The Farm and Home Units which were made responsible for the entire rural broadcast output, are headed by Farm Radio Officer. Besides, there are one or two Farm Radio Reporters and an Assistant Editor (Scripts).

The scope and structure of Farm and Home broadcasts have since changed and enlarged to meet the diversified needs and interests of the rural audience which grew in size over the years since independence. The objectives of Farm and Home broadcasts have transformed into the following:

(i) To inform the farming community about the latest scientific techniques of increasing crop and animal production.

(ii) To inform the non-agricultural rural population about the subsidiary and agro-based enterprises for improving their earnings.

(iii) To help the rural people participate in constructive agricultural and social programmes for betterment of rural life.

(iv) To inform the rural women on improved home making, on supporting their male counterparts on improved farming and to encourage them to participate in decision making for progress of scientific farming.

The quarterly programme schedules are prepared by the Farm Radio Officers which are discussed in the quarterly meetings of the Rural Programme Advisory Committees.

Officials of various development departments of the State Government, Agricultural University, non-official members like farmers and social workers are members of the committee. Vigilence is kept on the balance of subjects covered relating to agriculture and other aspects of rural development, the thrust areas and needs of the farmers during the quarter.

The Farm and Home units broadcast programmes on agriculture, horticulture, animal husbandry, poultry, fisheries, social forestry, agricultural marketing and agro-weather conditions. Stress is given on providing on a continuing basis the hints on modern agricultural practices, information on the cultivation of high yielding crop varieties and scientific methods of farming, soil and water management, fertiliser application, plant protection, harvesting techniques, storage and marketing and farm operation planning according to the weather conditions. The Units also provide active support to the development projects for small farmers marginal farmers and agricultural labourers, drought-prone areas and to Intensive Cattle Development Programme, High-yielding Variety Programme, Multiple Cropping Programme, National Demonstration Programme, Farmers Training and Functional Literacy Programme, Applied Nutrition Programme, Small Scale and Cottage Industries Programme, Integrated Child Development Programme, Maternal and Childcare Programme, Family Welfare Programme etc. The national programme of Poverty Alleviation of rural people gets extensive coverage. The programmes for rural women include information on nutrition, health and hygiene, maternal and childcare, home management, handicrafts, and on participation of women in dairy, poultry, duckery, goatery, fishery, storage of food grains, economic entrepreneurship etc. The programmes for rural children aim at encouraging them to inculcate practices and lifestyles to beçome aim at encouraging them to inculcate practices and lifestyles to become efficient citizens of the country.

Field Recording for Radio Broadcast

A decision on field recording may be made in two ways—(a) extension worker approaches the Farm Radio Officer and request for field recording to which he agrees, or (b) the Farm Radio Officer of his own requests for a field recording. The recording is done by the Farm Radio Officer or his staff and the extension worker has to attain his objectives by facilitating the process. The duration for broadcast of field recording may be for about 10 to 20 minutes. Recording should be done in such a way that it ensures clarity and vividness in broadcasting.

Objectives

(i) To motivate farmers and homemakers by highlighting achievements of other farmers and homemakers or research stations.

(ii) To provide information on extension activities like training programme, field day, exhibition, *Krishi mela* etc.

(iii) To provide information on the functioning of institutions and organisations in rural development.

(iv) To provide people with glimpses of rural life and how to improve it.

Techniques Used

Planning and Preparation

(i) Decide with the Farm Radio Officer on the topic, location and persons to be involved. For recording on technology transfer programme, involve one or two relevant scientists.

(ii) Also decide on the date, time, itinerary, conveyance and other details.

(iii) Inform the participants well in advance. Spot out some persons who have good voice and can clearly represent the facts.

(iv) Depending on the distance to be covered, keep not more than two or three spots to be covered in a single day's recording.

(v) Select suitable places, away from undesirable sound and distractions, where the recording may be done peacefully.

(vi) Decide on the major thrust to be made for each topic in each location. Prepare a script outlining the main points. If necessary, rehearse with the participants in advance.

(vii) Make simple but adequate arrangements for seating.

Implementation

(i) Take the Farm Radio Officer or his staff to the spot of recording in time.

(ii) Make the participants seated as needed for recording.

(iii) Make a quick discussion with the Farm Radio Officer and the participants about the message to be highlighted. Make all people feel at ease.

(iv) Take precaution against outside interference at the time of recording.

(v) See that the main theme has been brought out and recorded in an understandable and interesting way.

(vi) Use standard weights and measures so that they convey the same meaning to all the listeners.

(vii) If needed or requested by the Farm Radio Officer,

the extension worker may give his own voice for a short but pertinent information.

Follow-up

(i) Obtain date of broadcast from the radio station and communicate the same to the participants.

(ii) Display the date, time and topic of broadcast in the information centre of office of the extension worker.

(iii) Inform and encourage as many persons as possible to listen to the programmes.

(iv) Reply to the queries of the farmers as a result of the broadcast.

Limitations

(i) Lack of radio receiving sets may hinder communications.

(ii) No control of the extension worker over radio broadcast.

(iii) Generalised recommendations may limit their applicability.

Delivering a Talk or Discussing a Topic Over the Radio

The Farm Radio Officer may invite the extension worker or the specialist to deliver a straight talk or discuss a topic with other participants over the radio. The other participants may be some other extension workers, specialists, farmers, media-men etc. The total number of participants may be around 3 to 5. The duration for broadcast of straight talk may be around 5 to 10 minutes, while for discussion it may be around 10 to 20 minutes.

Objectives

(i) To convey an important message.

(ii) To emphasise a particular point.

Techniques Used

Planning and Preparation

(i) Develop a clear thinking on the topic.

(ii) Assemble relevant facts and data.

(iii) Consult research, if required.

(iv) Decide on the particular orientation and how it will be concluded.

Implication

(i) Prepare the script with a brief introduction, followed by the body of the talk, unfolding logically and step by step, and ending with a clear-cut conclusion. The script should be in a form as if the extension worker is talking to the audience and not reading out from a text.

(ii) Revise the draft twice or thrice until you are satisfied that nothing is to be added or deleted.

(iii) Arrange the write-up in short paragraphs, which shall facilitate giving pause at appropriate place at the time of recording.

(iv) Contact the Farm Radio Officer and get the script approved in advance. Revise the write-up if needed, according to his suggestions.

(v) A good script has the following characteristics—based on the needs of the people, presented in an interesting way, educative and has clarity.

(vi) Rehearse and find out whether the talk can be completed 1 to 2 minutes earlier than the time allotted. Be careful that there is not fumbling.

(vii) Reach the Radio Station on the appointed date and time. Remain seated there calmly till you are invited to the mike. Avoid any type of excitement.

(viii) At the time of recording, deliver the talk **calmly** and quietly in a good voice, with appropriate modulation and pause. The whole thing should appear as if you are talking to the audience and not reading out from a text.

For discussion programmes:

(i) Write down the important points to be discussed and arrange them logically.

(ii) Prepare brief notes explaining each of the points.

(iii) On the appointed date and time at the Radio Station, sit down with other participants and exchange views.

(iv) Decide which points shall be covered by whom and who shall speak after whom. Rehearse the whole discussion once or twice. Guard against dominant role of one or two persons.

(v) Check whether the intended message has been clearly brought out and the discussion is completed within the allotted time.

(vi) Do not bring any controversial issue at the discussion.

(vii) When invited at the mike, be seated in a sequence so that there is no confusion at the time of recording.

(viii) At the time of recording only one person shall speak at a time. Nobody should make an attempt to talk when the other person is speaking.

(ix) Bring out a lively discussion which the audience would like to listen.

Radio Rural Forum

A combination of mass media and inter-personal communication is more effective in reaching people with new ideas and persuade them to adopt innovations than mass media alone. Such combinations are known as media forums, where small organised groups of individuals meet regularly to receive a mass media programme and discuss its contents. Media forums developed originally in Canada among farm families and later spread to India, Nigeria, Ghana, Malawai, Costa Rica and Brazil.

In India, an experiment called Radio Rural Forums was sponsored jointly by the Ministry of Information and Broadcasting and the UNESCO in 1956. The forum members listened to bi-weekly broadcasts of the All India Radio for a duration of about 30-45 minutes each day, on agriculture and related subjects, held post-broadcast discussions and forwarded their queries to be answered by the original broadcaster or the expert. The forum has a chairman, a convenor, and is composed of 12-20 members. The convenor who acts as secretary, keeps record of attendance and writes the report in the prescribed form, seeking answers to queries and follow-up action proposed to be taken on the message. There is a District organiser on Radio Rural Forums, appointed by the State Government, who receives copies of the report sent to the radio station. The scheme was successful and was extended to the whole country. It was in its peak in the sixties, thereafter it declined, particularly after the winding up of the subsidised community listening scheme. The *Charcha Mandals* under the farmers' training programme, organised by the Ministry for Agriculture, also acted as forums.

Neurath (1960) made comparisons of increase in knowledge among peasants in three types of Indian villages—those in which radio forums were established, those in which radios were present but no forums were organised and those with neither a radio nor a forum. It was found that villages in which radio forums were organised, farmers had greater gain in knowledge of innovations, than in control villages. In fact, the non-forum villages with radio showed only very slight gain in knowledge. The results suggested that the effects of mass media channels, especially among peasants in less developed countries, are greater when these media are coupled with interpersonal communication channels in media forums.

The reasons for the media having greater effects on individuals when they are members of media forums are—

(i) Interest in attendance and participation is encouraged by group pressure and social expectations.
(ii) Attitude change is readily achieved when individuals are in groups.
(iii) Group decisions are more likely to be accepted by the individual if he participates in making decision, as usually occurs in media forums.
(iv) High credibility of the medium (in this case the All India Radio) may account for some of the success of the media forums.

Farm School on the Air

Farm School is a method of providing systematic education on farming to the farmers through the process of distance learning. The following are the steps involved in the broadcast of Farm School:

(i) Planning of a comprehensive syllabus through selection of topics by a Subject Committee composed of Farm Radio Officer and experts of the Department of Agriculture of the State Government and Agriculture University.
(ii) Selection of the trainer by the Subject Committee to prepare the lessons on the selected topic and to deliver them over radio.

(iii) Structuring a series of lessons, usually 15-20 on every topic, by the trainer and approval of the lessons by the Subject Committee.

(iv) Registration of names by the trainee listeners with the radio station and announcement of registration numbers.

(v) Broadcast of lessons by the trainer on pre-announced fixed days, once every week, with provision for repeat broadcasts.

(vi) Lecture-cum-discussion-cum-question-answer format is used and training session in the studio is participated by the trainer, an extension worker and a few farmers.

(vii) Broadcast of the summary and relevant questions with answers from the trainer at the end of each lesson.

(viii) Trainee listeners mail answer sheets containing answers to the questions broadcast on each lesson.

(ix) Trainer evaluates the answer sheets and assigns marks.

(x) Announcement of results over radio and issue of certificates of participation by the radio station to the trainee farmers.

(xi) Award of prizes ceremoniously to the meritorious trainees.

In order to reach the education to illiterate and farmers not owning radio sets, quiz contests as part of the Farm School are arranged. The successful trainee listeners are invited to form their groups each of 3-4 non-trainee illiterate farmers. The groups contest in the quiz. Thus, Farm School trainees are utilised to spread the farm education they obtain from the Farm School.

7. Television

Television is an electronic audio-visual medium which provides pictures with words and sound effects. This medium is cosmopolite in approach and can be used to create instant mass awareness. It can deal with topical problems and provide solutions. The contributes information and speeds up the process of adoption. Television is strong in providing the stimulus, and exposing the audience to a whole range of ideas and experiences.

In comparison to motion picture, television can create more impact due to its flexibility, less time taken to record and telecast programmes and wider coverage. Compared to radio, television has, however, less impact in rural India, mainly because of low availability of this medium due to high cost of receiving sets. Coverage of more area by increasing the transmission facility of television does not necessarily indicate the availability of this medium to the rural audience. Availability of cheap receiving sets which may be operated with electricity or battery, increased frequency of telecast and more effective programmes can bring a real breakthrough in the utilisation of this medium by the rural audience.

Farm Telecasts

According to a report complied by the Research and Reference Division of the Ministry of Information and Broadcasting (1984) the television era in India began modestly on September 15, 1959 by a UNESCO grant to study the use of TV as a medium of education, rural uplift and community development. The service was operated by the All India Radio, from a small improvised studio in Delhi and programmes were telecast twice a week for a duration of one hour each day. It was a transmission mainly for urban viewers although the range of reception was 24 km. covering many village around the capital. Teleclubs were organised for community viewing. In 1967 came the pilot project of agricultural communication initiated by Dr. Vikram Sarabhai. The programme titled *Krishi Darshan* was primarily aimed at demonstrating the effectiveness of TV as a medium for propagating improved farming practices. With the introduction of agricultural improved farming practices. With the introduction of agricultural programmes, a number of teleclubs were organised in the rural areas.

Satellite Instructional Television Experiment (SITE) transmissions were inaugurated on August 15, 1975 reaching 2,400 villages in the backward areas of the States of Andhra Pradesh, Bihar, Karnataka, Madhya Pradesh, Orissa and Rajasthan representing a wide range of linguistic, cultural, climatic and agricultural regions of the country. Each selected village was provided with a Direct Reception Set (DRS) and to cater to the unelectrified villages battery operated sets were installed. The period of experiment was one year.

With the extensive social research and evaluation, establishing the unique usefulness of TV as an effective medium of communication in the most vulnerable areas, the Government decided to continue transmission to at least 40 per cent of the villages after the completion of SITE programme, through terrestrial transmitters.

In July 1983, The Government took up a crash programme under INSAT for promotion of agricultural productivity. Specified clusters in six States, Andhra Pradesh, Bihar, Gujarat, Maharashtra, Orisa and Uttar Pradesh were identified on the basis of backwardness of the area, availability of suitable physical and developmental infrastructure and utilisation of the existing TV programme production facilities. With increased capability of satellite communication and TV transmission in India, telecast of agricultural and rural development programmes are being organised in a big way.

Objectives

(i) To create general awareness about agricultural and rural development programmes.
(ii) To provide need based programme to the rural audience.
(iii) To show the rural people in general, and the farmers in particular, what to do, how to do and with what result.

The Producer, Agricultural Programmes of the television station is in charge of the agricultural and rural programmes. The television programmes with which the extension worker is concerned may be of three types—publicising extension programmes, field recording of specific extension activities and achievement, and recording of research based and 'how to do' type programmes. For any type of programme, an appointment is to be made well in advance with the Producer, Agricultural Programmes. For publicising extension programmes, elaborate preparation is not needed, except making arrangements for transport where required. Training programmes, field day, exhibition, campaign, seminar, symposium, workshop etc. which have got some news value, are generally covered under this programme. These are generally telecast along with the news and not in the slot provided for agricultural and rural programmes.

For field recording of specific extension activities and achievements, and recording research based and 'how to do' type programmes, the extension worker has to do a lot.

Video System

Television operates on video system. This has two sub-systems—video recording system and video player system. The systems have the following main components.

Video Recording System—

(i) Video Camera
(ii) Video Cassette Recorder (VCR)
(iii) Microphone

Video Player System —

(i) Video Cassette Player (VCP)
(ii) Television.

The function of the video recording system is to prepare video tapes. The picture is taken by the video camera and the sound is picked up by the microphone, which are recorded on the video tapes by the video cassette recorder.

The VCR may also be used as VCP. Where video tapes are not required to be made, and pre-recorded video cassettes are used, a VCP will do. For playing, the video cassette is put into the VCP and its player output is put into the TV input and the system is switched on. A source of energy, either compact rechargeable battery or electricity is needed to put the system in operation.

REFERENCES

Baruah, U.L. (1983), *This is All India Radio: A Handbook of Radio Broadcasting in India*. Publications Division, Ministry of Information and Broadcasting. Govt. of India, New Delhi.

Behrens J.H. and Evans J.F. (1984), Using Mass Media for Extension Teaching, in (ed.) *Agricultural Extension: A Reference Manual,* Swanson B.D. FAO, Rome.

Leagans J.P. (1961), *Extension Teaching Methods,* in *Extension Education in Community Development.* Directorate of Extension, Ministry of Food and Agriculture, Govt. of India, New Delhi.

Neurath Paul (1960), *Radio Farm Forum in India.* Govt. of India Press, Delhi.

Reddy A.A. (1987), *Extension Education.* Sree Lakshmi Press, Bapatla, Andhra Pradesh.

APPENDIX—I

CODE OF ATHENS

International Code of Ethics for Public Relations

Considering that all Member Countries of the United Nations Organisation have agreed to abide by its Charter which reaffirms 'its faith in fundamental human rights, in the dignity and worth of the human person' and that having regarding to the very nature of their profession, Public Relations practitioners in these countries should undertake to ascertain and observe the principles set out in this Charter.

Considering that apart from 'rights', human beings have not only physical or material needs but also intellectual, moral and social needs, and that their rights are of real benefit to them only insofar as these needs are essentially met.

Considering that, in the course of their professional duties and depending on how these dudes are performed, Public Relations practitioners can substantially help to meet these intellectual, moral and social needs.

And lastly, considering that the use of techniques enabling them to come simultaneously into contract with millions of people gives Public Relations practitioners a power that has to be restrained by the observance of a strict moral code.

On all these grounds the undersigned. Public Relations Associations hereby declare that they accept, as their moral charter the principles of the following Code of Ethics, and that if the light of evidence submitted to the Society a member of these Associations should be found to have infringed this Code in the course of his professional duties, he will be deemed to be guilty of serious misconduct calling for an appropriate penalty.

Accordingly, each Member of these Associations:

Shall Endeavour

1. To contribute to the achievement of the moral and cultural conditions enabling human beings to reach their full stature and enjoy the indefeasible rights to which they are entitled under the 'Universal Declaration of Human Rights';
2. To establish communication patterns and channels which, by fostering the free flow of essential information, will make each member of the society in which he lives feel that he is being kept informed and also give him an awareness of his own personal involvement and responsibility and of his solidarity with other members;
3. To bear in mind that, because of the relationship between his profession and the public, his conduct,— even in private—will have an impact on the way in which the profession as a whole is appraised;
4. To respect, in the course of his professional duties, the moral principles and rules of the 'Universal Declaration of Human Rights';
5. To pay due regard to, and uphold, human dignity, and to recognise the right of each individual to judge for himself;
6. To encourage the moral, psychological and intellectual conditions for dialogue in its true sense and to recognise the right of the parties involved to state their case and express their views;

Shall Undertake

7. To conduct himself always and in all circumstances in such a manner as to deserve and secure the confidence of those with whom he comes into contact;
8. To act in all circumstances, in such a manner as to take account of the respective interests of the parties involved: both the interests of the organisation which he serves and the interests of the publics concerned;
9. To carry out his duties with integrity, avoiding language likely to lead to ambiguity or misunderstanding, and to maintain loyalty to his clients or employers, whether past of present.

Shall Refrain From

10. Subordinating the truth to other requirements;
11. Circulating information, which is not based on established and ascertainable facts;
12. Taking part in any venture or undertaking which is unethical or dishonest or capable of impairing human dignity and integrity;
13. Using any 'manipulative' methods or techniques designed to create subconscious motivations which the individual cannot control of his own free will and so cannot be held accountable for the action taken on them.

APPENDIX—II

CODE OF PROFESSIONAL CONDUCT OF THE INSTITUTE OF PUBLIC RELATIONS—U.K.

This Code defines and implements! paragraph, 3(a) (ii) of the Memorandum of the Institute of Public Relations under the heading 'Objects', namely 'to encourage and foster the observance of high professional standards by its members and to establish and prescribed such standards'. Public relations is concerned with the effect of conduct on reputation. The following principles have been laid down to embody this concept and enhance relations between the Institute's members and the public to whom they are directly or indirectly responsible in the performance of their duties.

1. A member shall conduct his professional activities with respect for the public interest.
2. A member shall at all times deal fairly and honestly with his client or employers past and present, with his fellow members, and with the general public.
3. A member shall not intentionally disseminate false or misleading information, and shall use proper care to avoid doing so. He has a positive duty to maintain truth, accuracy, and good taste.
4. A member shall not engage in any practice which tends to corrupt the integrity of channels of public communication.
5. A member shall not create or make use of any organisation purporting to serve some announced cause but actually promoting a special or private interest of a member or his client or his employer which is not apparent.

6. A member shall safeguard the confidences of both present and former clients or employers. He shall not disclose except upon the order of a court of competent jurisdiction any confidential information which he may have obtained in his official capacity without securing and making known the consent of the said client or employer.
7. A member shall not represent conflicting or competing interests without the express consent of those concerned given after full disclosure of the facts.
8. A member in performing services for a client or employer shall not accept fees, commissions or any other valuable consideration in connection with those services from anyone other than his client or employer unless such practice is acceptable to the client or employer.
9. A member shall not cause or allow to be done anything for the purpose of touting or advertising calculated to attract business unfairly.
10. A member shall not propose to a prospective client or employer that his fee or other compensation be contingent on the achievement of certain results; nor shall he enter into any fee agreement to the same effect.
11. A member shall not intentionally injure the professional reputation or practice of another member, but if such a member has evidence that another has been guilty of unethical, illegal or unfair practices it, shall be his duty to inform the Institute in accordance with the Memorandum and Articles.
12. A member shall not engage in or be connected with, any occupation or business which, in the

opinion of the Council, is not consistent with membership of the Institute.

13. A member shall not seek to supplant another member with his employer or client, nor shall he encroach upon the professional employment of another member unless both parties are assured that there is no conflict of interest involved and are kept advise of the negotiations.
14. A member shall cooperate with fellow members in upholding and enforcing this Code.

APPENDIX—III

INTERNATIONAL CODE OF ETHICS FOR PUBLIC RELATIONS AND ADOPTED BY THE PUBLIC RELATIONS SOCIETY OF INDIA AT ITS 1ST NATIONAL CONFERENCE AT NEW DELHI ON 21.4.1968

Considering that all Member countries of the United Nations Organisation have agreed to abide by its Charter which reaffirm "its faith in fundamental human rights, in the dignity and worth of he human person" and that have regard to the very nature of their profession, Public Relations practitioners in these countries should undertake to ascertain and observe the principles set out in this Charter,

Considering that apart from "rights", human beings have not only physical or material needs but also intellectual, moral and social needs, and that their rights are of real benefit to them only insofar as these needs are essentially met,

Considering that, in the course of their professional duties and depending on how these duties are performed, Public Relations practitioners can substantially help to meet these intellectual, moral and social needs,

And lastly, Considering that the use of techniques enabling them to come simultaneously into contact with millions of people gives Public Relations practitioners a power that has to be restrained by the observance of a strict moral code,

On all these grounds, the Public Relations Society of India hereby declares that it accepts, as its moral charter the principle of the following Code of Ethics, and that if, in the light of evidence submitted to the Society, a member of this Society should be found to have infringed this

Code in the course of his professional duties, he will be deemed to be guilty of serious misconduct calling for an appropriate penalty.

Accordingly, each Member of this Society

1. To contribute to the achievement of the moral and cultural conditions enabling human beings to reach their full stature and enjoy the indefeasible rights to which they are entitled under the "Universal Declaration of Human Rights";
2. To establish communication patterns and channels which, by fostering the free flow of essential information, will make each member of the group feel that he is being kept informed, and also give him an awareness of his own personal involvement and responsibility and of his solidarity with other members;
3. To conduct himself always and in all circumstances in such a manner as to deserve and secure the confidence of those with whom he comes into contact;
4. To bear in mind that, because of the relationship between his profession and the public, his conduct—even in private—will have an impact on the way in which the profession as a whole is appraised;

Shall undertake

5. To observe, in the course of his professional duties, the moral principles and rules of the "Universal Declaration of Human Rights";
6. To pay due regard to, and uphold, human dignity, and to recognise the right of each individual to judge for himself;

7. To establish the moral, psychological and intellectual conditions for dialogue in its true sense, and to recognise the right of the parties involved to state their case and express their views;
8. To act, in all circumstances in such a manner as to take account of the respective interest of the parties involved: both the interests of the organisation which he services and the interests of the publics concerned;
9. To carry out his undertakings and commitments which shall always be so worded as to avoid any misunderstanding, and to show loyalty and integrity in all circumstances so as to keep the confidence of his clients or employers, past or present, and of all the publics that are affected by his actions;

Shall Refrain From

10. Subordinating the truth to other requirements;
11. Circulating information which is not based on established and ascertainable facts;
12. Taking part in any venture or undertaking which is unethical or dishonest or capable of impairing human dignity and integrity;
13. Using any "manipulative" methods or techniques designed to create subconscious motivations which the individual cannot control of his own free will and so cannot be held accountable for the action taken on them.

APPENDIX—IV

CODE OF PROFESSIONAL STANDARDS

This code of professional standards for the practice of public relations is adopted by the Public Relations Society of America to promote and maintain high standards of public service and conduct among its members. As such: membership in the society can be deemed a badge of ethical conduct; public relations may be justly regarded as a profession; the public can have increasing confidence in the field's integrity; and the practice of public relations will best serve the public interest.

1. A member has a general duty of fair dealing toward clients or employers (past and present), fellow members, and the general public,
2. A member's professional life will be conducted in accord with the public welfare.
3. A member has the affirmative duty of adhering to generally accepted standards of accuracy, truth, and good taste.
4. A member shall not represent conflicting or competing interests without the express consent of those concerned given after a full disclosure of the facts.
5. A member shall safeguard the confidence of both present and former clients or employers and shall not accept retainers or employment that may involve the disclosure or use of these confidences to the disadvantage or prejudice of such clients or employers.
6. A member shall not engage in any practice that tends to corrupt the integrity of channels of public communication.

7. A member shall not intentionally disseminate false or misleading information and is obligated to use ordinary care to avoid dissemination of false or misleading information.
8. A members hall not make use of any organisation purporting to serve some announced cause but actually serving an undisclosed special or private interest of a member, a client or employer.
9. A member shall not intentionally injure the professional reputation or practice of another member. However, if a member has evidence that another member has been guilty of unethical, illegal, or unfair practices, including practices in violation of this code, that member shall present the information to the proper authorities of the society for action in accordance with the procedure set forth in Article XIII of the Bylaws.
10. A member shall not employ methods tending to be derogatory of another member's client or employer or the products, business, or services of such client or employer.
11. In employing services for a client or employer, a member shall not accept fee, commission, or other valuable consideration in connection with these services from anyone other than the client or employer without the express consent of the client or employer, given after a full disclosure of the facts.
12. A member shall not propose to a prospective client or employer that the fee or other compensation is contingent on the achievement of certain results; nor shall the member enter into any fee agreement to the same effect.

13. A member shall not encroach upon the professional employment of another member unless both are assured that there is no conflict between the two engagements and are kept advised of the negotiations.
14. A member shall, as soon as possible, sever relations with any organisation when continued employment with that organisation would require conduct contrary to the provisions of this code.
15. A member called as a witness in a proceeding for the enforcement of this code shall be bound to appear unless, for sufficient reasons, the member shall be excused by the panel hearing the same.
16. A member shall cooperate with fellow members in upholding and enforcing this code.

This code offers a sound ethical framework for all people practising public relations today. Additionally, it provides organisations with a clear declaration of the kind of standards it should seek in hiring internal practitioners and in employing outside counsels.

APPENDIX—V

WHAT IS EXPECTED OF PUBLIC RELATIONS PRACTITIONERS

1. Counseling based on an understanding of human behaviour.
2. Analysing present and future trends and predicting their consequences.
3. Research into public opinion, attitudes and expectations and advising on necessary action.
4. Establishing and maintaining two-way communication based on truth, honesty and full information.
5. Preventing conflict and misunderstanding.
6. Promoting mutual respect and social responsibility.
7. Harmonising the private and the public interest.
8. Promoting good-wilt with employees, suppliers and customers.
9. Improving industrial relations.
10. Attracting good personnel, reducing labour turnover and promoting productivity.
11. Promotion of products, services and exports.
12. Maximising profitability.
13. Projecting a corporate identity, and helping in the building up of a corporate culture.
14. Encouraging an active and lively interest in international affairs.
15. Promoting an understanding of democracy and values of freedom at national and international levels.

Glossary of Terms

Account

A client of a public relations or advertising agency.

Animation

A motion picture production from drawings, each successive drawing showing a very slight change of position so that a series of themgive the effect of definite movement.

Audit Bureau of Circulation

The organisation sponsored by publishers, agencies, and advertisers to secure accurate circulation statements.

Brainstorming

The creative process of group thinking about and articulating ideas on a given subject or problem generally recorded for future evaluation and use.

Broadcast

The dissemination of programmes or messages by radio or television.

Brochure

Usually refers to a printed piece containing six or more pages.

Byline

Name of the writer positioned under the headline at the beginning of the story.

Cable TV

Distant and interference-free images received on a TV

screen by means of wires rather than by means of an antenna receiving signals from a broadcast station.

Client

The organisation or person who retains an outside agency for specialised services.

Closed Circuit TV

Live videotape or film material transmittedby cable for private viewing on a TV monitor.

Communication

The art of transmitting information, ideas and attitudes from one person to another through verbal and/or visual symbols. Requires sender, message and receiver.

Content Analysis

The technique of reading publications/advertisements/ messages to find references to an organisation or an idea, then coding and analysing the content to determine trends andopinions.

Contingency Plan

A written plan of activities prepared in advance to be put into effect only if certain specified events occur.

Corporate Colour

Colour authorised for use in corporate logo.

Corporate Communication

The entire range of public relations activities of a corporation as a whole, rather than activities designed for its individual segments.

Corporate Typeface

Approved typeface for use in the corporated identity programme.

Created Event

An event or occasion created by public relations personnel to attract news coverage.

Data

Raw facts or observations; factual material used as a basis for discussion ordecision-making.

Deadline

The day and hour by which news copy must be in the hands of the editor of a newspaper or broadcast/ telecast producer.

Direct Mail

The promotion of ideas, products or services by letters or advertising sent to carefully selected lists of people.

Editorial

An expression of the views and opinions of the management of a publication or broad-casting operation.

Embargo

The warning about publication of a news release on a specified date, usually appears at the top of the first page of the news release or statement

Employee Communication

The two-way transmission of information to and from management and employees by various media, letters, newsletters, magazines etc.

Evaluation

Measurement of success or failure of a programme or a concept.

Exclusive

A news story offered by a public relations practitioner to a single newspaper, broadcast or television station.

Exposure

The extent to which the target audience becomes aware of a person, activity, theme or organisation from the efforts of PR or advertising.

Feature Article

A newspaper or magazine article which discusses and interprets an event or trends as opposed to spot reporting.

Film Strip

A visual aid consisting of a short strip of firm on which individually projected pictures are printed, generally synchronised with a sound track or audio tape.

Financial Public Relations

The efforts of a publicly held company to communicate with shareholders, security analysts, institutional investors, stock exchanges etc.

Format

The size, make-up and general appearance of a publication.

Fourth Estate

Generally identified with the Press. Derived from England where the Lords Temporal(House of Lords), the Lord Spiritual (the Clergy) and the House of Commons occupy the three "estates of the realm". Looking at the clout the press enjoyed it was recognised that the press was the Fourth Estate.

Gatekeepers

A jargon used for people or groups who filter information in a communication network. Also referred to as opinion leaders, they accept or reject a message before it reaches the public. Gatekeepers exert great influence. In a newspaper or periodical, the term refers to the person

(News Editor Chief Subeditior) who decides what news is to be used and what not.

Going Public

The process by which a company issues and sells stock to the public, thus converting it to a public limited company.

Grapevine

Slang used for information passed among employees that has not been officially circulated by the company.

House Journal

A company publication aimed at its employees and/ or other target groups. It can be internal, external, or a combination of the two. Also known as house magazine, house organ or newsletter.

Indepth Interview

A lengthy technique requiring skill that gauges both conscious and unconscious perceptions and motivations.

Institutional Advertising

Paid advertising that promotes the company and its ideas or policies rather than its products and services.

Interviewer

The individual who asks respondents the questions specified in a questionnaire of a survey.

Leaflet

A printed piece, usually with four to six folds, for inexpensive distribution.

Libel

Printing or broadcasting a false or defamatory statement that injures a person's feelings or reputation.

Logo

A graphic symbol or combination of symbols and stylised letters forming an acronym.

Management

The people charged with the responsibility of determining organisational or corporate policies and planning and directing its operations.

Media Relations

The relationship between the company and all the various media of communication, including print and electronic.

Media

The mass communication outlets available for the transmission of messages. The media include newspapers, magazines, radio, television etc.

Mileage

A slang used to refer to the number of column inches obtained in the print media on a given subject being publicised.

Muckrakers

A term used for journalists who seek out and expose scandals or supposed scandals with unworthy motives.

News Conference

A gathering of members of the news media, both print and broadcast, to cover an announcement usually too complicated to convey in any other manner.

News Release

A written communication usually containing information of a timely nature sent to all news media.

Open House

An occasion when a company invites its employees, customers, suppliers, or neighbours to visit the factory. Senior managers generally circulate among the guests.

Opinion Polls

Research based on the theory of probability, generally conducted with questionnaires to ascertain the attitudes and opinions of a particular section of the community, public.

Pamphlet

Almost synonymous with booklet or brochure.

Press Junket

A facility visit for media representatives in which transportation, accommodation and other facilities are provided so they can view a special event or visit a site for reporting.

Press Kit

Usually a docket containing background material, photographs, illustrations and news releases distributed at a news conference as source materials for the news media.

Prestige Advertising

Advertising that tends to build an image or reputation rather than sell a specific product or service. It is in fact another term for institutional advertising.

Proactive Public Relations

Suo moto public relations anticipating events, circumstances, or situations, often through the execution of contingency plans; basically planned and aggressive public relations.

Proof

An impression of composed type in ink for marking corrections.

Propaganda

Originally meant to spread a belief, propagate an idea, now used to denote promoting true or false ideas to make converts.

Public Affairs

Usually refers to an organisation's relations with government and legislative bodies.

Public Relations

Planned, organised and sustained programme to develop public confidence and increase understanding towards an organisation.

Public Service Advertising

Advertising with a message in the public interest.

Publicity

Information about an individual organisation, event, issue or product disseminated through various media of mass communication to attract attention and influence opinion.

Reactive Public Relations

A policy of responding to a given set of circumstances, situations or events after the fact. Basically defensive Public Relations.

Reinforcement

To strengthen the attitudes and opinions of those who already tend to agree with or are committed to a given cause.

Respondent

The individual who is questioned and who responds to survey questions.

Rumour

A widely circulated, unverified and usually inaccurate story from an unknown source.

Sample

A portion of the total population involved in a survey. Although relatively small, if scientifically drawn, this portion is representative of the total population involved.

Satellite

A communication satellite by means of which messages are relayed to and from earth stations.

Slides

A visual aid making use of pictures projected on to a screen.

Sound Slide

Visual illustrations projected on a screen simultaneously with a record or sound tape.

Source

A person with useful information to communicate and who is contacted 1 by the media.

Special Event

A situation or happening designed to influence opinion, such as an anniversary, reception, grand opening, sporting event, product introduction etc.

Synergisra

The action of two elements that when mixed have a greater impact than the sum of the two acting independently.

Targets

Any primary group/audience to be reached with a message—like teachers, farmers, scientists, employees, shareholders et al.

Trade Mark

A work or design used on an article of merchandise to identify it as the product of a particular manufacturer like the Tatas, Hindustan Lever, Steel Authority of India, Bharat Heavy Electricals etc.

Select Bibliography

Alien Fred T., *Ways to Improve Employee Communication,* National Business, September, 1975, pp. 54-56.

Baruah, U.L. (1983), *This is All India Radio: A Handbook of Radio Broadcasting in India.* Publications Division, Ministry of Information and Broadcasting. Govt. of India, New Delhi.

Bateman J. Carroll, *Public Relations for Business and Professional Association.*

Behrens J.H. and Evans J.F. (1984), Using Mass Media for Extension Teaching, in (ed.) *Agricultural Extension: A Reference Manual,* Swanson B.D. FAO, Rome.

D.M. Silvera, *Human Resource Development, The Indian Experience,* News India Publication, 1988, New Delhi.

Fraser P. Seitel, Charles E., *The Practice of Public Relations,* Merrill Publishing Co, A Bell & Howell Company, Columbus, Ohio.

Gadgil, D.R. (1965), *Planning and Economic Policy in India,* Poona, Gokhale Institute of Politics and Economics.

John, Wilmshurst, *The Fundamentals of Advertising.*

King, J.A. (Jr.) (1967), *Economic Development Projects and Their Appraisal,* Baltimore, Johns Hopkins Press.

Kolter, Philip *Marketing Management Analysis, Planning and Control,* Prentice Hall of India Pvt. Ltd., New Delhi.

Leagans J.P. (1961), *Extension Teaching Methods,* in *Extension Education in Community Development.* Directorate of Extension, Ministry of Food and Agriculture, Govt. of India, New Delhi.

Little, I.M.D. and Mirrlees, J.A. (1969), *Manual of Industrial Projects Analysis in Developing Countries.* Vol. II, Paris, Organisation for Economic Cooperation and Development

Mehta, D.S. (1992), "A Public Relations fob" *Hindustan Times,* Sunday-Supplement.

Merlye Davids and Michael Winklemn, "Blurred Vision," *PR Journal,* September, 1987.

Neurath Paul (1960), *Radio Farm Forum in India.* Govt. of India Press, Delhi.

Reddy A.A. (1987), *Extension Education.* Sree Lakshmi Press, Bapatla, Andhra Pradesh.

Rotman, Morris B. (1974), *'PR is Still Necessary Adjunct to Efficient Marketing Today'* Advertising & Sales Promotion.

Seitel, Fraser P. Charles E., *The Practice of Public Relations,* Merrill Publishing Co. A Bell & Howell Company, Columbus.

Tom Garbett, *Corporate Advertising*—the what, the why and how.

Zausner M., *Corporate Policy and Investment Community,* New York, Ronald Press, 1968.

Index